*Operating
the
Sheet-fed Offset
Press*

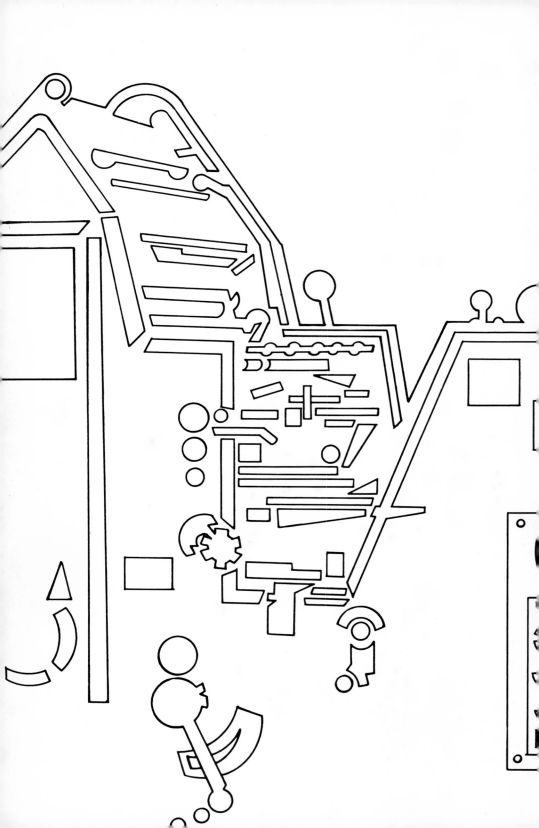

Operating the Sheet-fed Offset Press

Lane Olinghouse

North American Publishing Company
Philadelphia

to my wife
Gertrude Pierson Olinghouse
who appreciates the challenges
of offset printing
and of writing about it

Library of Congress Catalog Number: 75-25430
ISBN: 0-912920-44-0
Order Number: 135

Printed in the United States of America

Contents

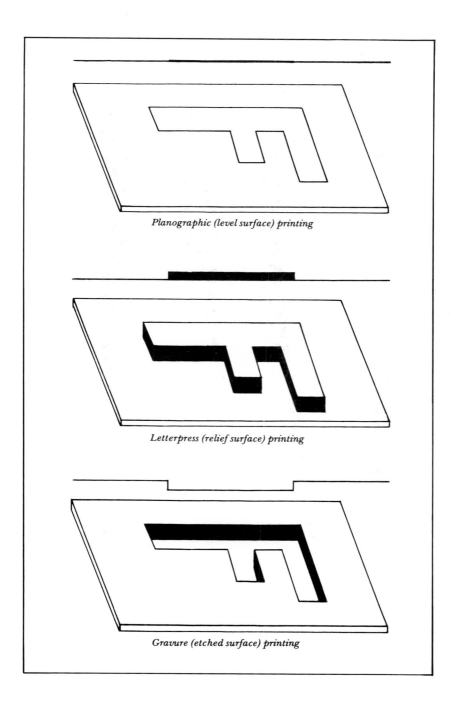

Planographic (level surface) printing

Letterpress (relief surface) printing

Gravure (etched surface) printing

Introduction
On Understanding
Offset Lithography

In order to run a modern offset printing press, the operator does not need to know all there is to know about the theory, the history or the development of this method of reproduction. Detailed instruction manuals designed to show the correct operating procedures for each type of machine and insure consistent production of acceptable-to-professional quality work guide the operator's every step. The person who commands a reasonably high degree of manual dexterity, and who can follow explicitly written directions, ordinarily experiences little difficulty with these water-and-ink machines. Nevertheless, the following material should prove both interesting and illuminating to the person recently introduced to the somewhat exotic craft of offset printing, or lithography.

The Beginnings

The ever-widening field of offset lithography comprises one of the basic types of planographic printing. These include stone lithography, direct lithography and collotype or photogelatin printing. Planographic refers to the fact that both image and non-image areas of the printing surface lie essentially on the same level or plane. In planographic printing, that part of the image carrier that does the printing is neither raised above the image carrier's surface as in letterpress printing, nor cut below the surface as in gravure printing. Offset lithography's position in the printing industry has become so well established in recent years that the terms offset lithography, offset printing and planographic printing now are practically synonymous.

Though the basic principles of lithography (litho: stone; graphos: writing) were understood and practiced 175 years ago by the followers and imitators of Austrian-born Alois Senefelder, it was not until about 1904 that Ira Rubel of Nutley, New Jersey, introduced offset lithographic printing of paper. Before then lithographic reproduction largely involved some method of direct printing, i.e., lithographic stone to paper.

In the early days of lithography, carefully cut and skillfully prepared Bavarian limestone provided both the image carrier and the printing surface. For the most part, methods of lithographic printing used then were slow and cumbersome. Stones of suitable size and characteristics were expensive and scarce. Senefelder's work with lithographic printing presses resulted in his introduction in 1813 of a flat, lightweight metal plate to replace the heavy stones. Later, further experimentation by others led to the use of flexible zinc and aluminum plates that could be wrapped around and secured to a cylindrical surface. Those first lithographic plates, though a definite improvement over the heavy stones, left much to be desired. Printing directly onto abrasive-surfaced papers, the metal plates had a relatively short image life.

Rubel's idea of interpositioning a rubber blanket between the image carrier or plate and the material being printed permitted indirect printing of the image via a non-abrasive surface. Working against the smooth, resilient surface of a flexible rubber blanket, the plate retained its image for a considerably longer time or greater number of impressions. The introduction of indirect or offset printing made long-run lithographic reproduction commercially feasible.

Many of the refinements found today in offset lithography are based on Rubel's achievement, which gave this form of printing its commonly accepted modifier "offset." Photography and the development of contact screens subsequently made it possible to reproduce both line drawings and halftone illustrations on the light-sensitive surface of the same plate.

The Lithographic Principle

The basic principle to grasp in understanding offset printing or lithography is that under controlled conditions oil, or greasy ink, and water will not mix. This makes it possible through chemical, photographic and mechanical treatment of specially prepared image carriers to provide a surface that tends to reject ink in certain selected (non-image) areas and accept ink in other (image) areas. Through this three-step treatment, the image or printing areas become both ink receptive and water repellant and the non-image or non-printing areas become ink repellant and water receptive.

It is only necessary, then, to find some means of supplying a continuous stream or film of water to the image carrier's surface at the same time a film of ink is being applied to the image area, in order to shield the non-image areas from the ink. The offset printing press, with its introduction of water and ink at the plate's surface through two separate roller systems, does this with an efficiency limited only by the skill of the operator and the physical and chemical laws of nature.

Moisture applied to the plate's surface adheres to the non-image areas of the plate. A plate developing ink applied to the plate by the platemaker prevents the moisture from adhering to the image or printing areas. The ink form rollers which next come in contact with the plate lay a film of ink on this ink-receptive image.

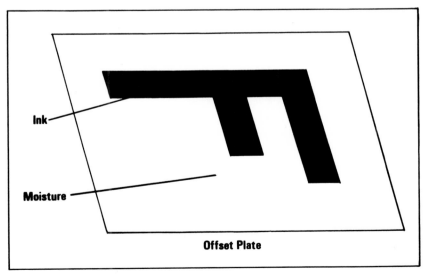

Moistened non-image areas on the photochemically treated offset plate reject ink while the image area accepts ink.

The moisture placed on the non-image areas of the plate prevents the film of ink from covering these portions of the plate's surface.

Successful utilization of the lithographic principle requires continuous control of both the inking and the dampening systems on the press. Unless the operator maintains a strict balance between the water and ink being applied to the plate's surface during each revolution of the press, difficulties peculiar to offset printing quickly develop.

One difficulty, water-in-ink emulsion, occurs when excess amounts of water or dampening solution admitted to the plate's surface break down the ink film's resistance to moisture. When this happens, molecules of water impregnate the film of ink, in direct violation of the rule that water and oil will not mix. The moisture-laden ink causes problems by refusing to adhere properly to the inking roller surfaces and to distribute evenly across the printing or image areas of the plate. The result is a deterioration of the printed image. Ink-in-water emulsion, a less frequent occurrence, results in a discoloration of the film of dampening solution; this causes a tint or shade of the ink to adhere to the non-image areas of the plate and show up on the printed sheets.

A second difficulty, called scumming, follows when the non-image areas of the plate begin to accept some of the ink directly. In this case, insufficient amounts of water or dampening solution are reaching the plate's surface. Without an adequately protective film of moisture, the non-image areas of the plate take up some of the ink from the inking rollers. Since both dampening rollers and inking rollers pass over the entire surface of the plate between 75 and 150 times each minute, any lack of ink resistance on the part of the non-image areas soon reveals itself in an inky smudge in these areas on the printed material.

Not all offset printing presses have inking and dampening systems that work exactly in this manner. On some presses the water, or fountain solution as it often is called, is applied to an intermediate inking roller instead of directly to the plate. One of the ink form rollers then applies both water and ink to the plate as it passes over the plate's surface. This type of ink/dampening system may present its own kind of problems to the operator.

In any case, the operator must keep the amounts of water and ink admitted to the image carrier within the limits dictated by the job in progress. Too much or too little of either can cause problems. Both dampening and inking systems must be set with care and the settings must be maintained or carefully adjusted throughout the job of printing. At all times the operator must avoid excessive, insufficient or uneven amounts of water and avoid excessive, insufficient or uneven amounts of ink in order to produce satisfactory work with the offset printing press.

Limitations and Advantages

Like all other presses, the sheetfed offset press has definite limitations of a physical or mechanical as well as a chemical nature. One such limitation involves the use of a plate or image carrier that prohibits repositioning of any of the elements of the image. If faulty stripping or platemaking procedures result in an impositioning error of some element of the image—a page, an illustration, a block of copy—the operator will have to request a replacement of the plate. Unless another job can be introduced conveniently in the intervening time, considerable press downtime can result from the operator's inability to reposition or correct even small portions of the image.

However, the essentially single-element image carrier also proves advantageous to the users of offset printing presses in two ways:

1. The individual elements of the image are assembled away from the press prior to printing; thus impositioning and platemaking procedures do not impinge on the time allotted to actual presswork.

2. It requires far less time to secure to the plate cylinder of an offset press the several elements of the image on a single plate than it does to install and lock up multiple-element image carriers on a letterpress.

Separating the assembling or page-impositioning tasks from presswork procedures offers several definite time-saving options. Occurring at a different stage of production, the assembling tasks involved can coincide with similar tasks for other jobs of printing.

The platemaker, for instance, can process plates for a number of different jobs in one platemaking session. And handling a single, lightweight, wrap-around image carrier instead of several relatively heavy and bulky forms allows the operator to perform installation and lockup tasks easier and faster with less press downtime. In most cases, the advantages of offset printing so far outweigh the disadvantages that this method of reproduction finds an ever-increasing number of enthusiastic supporters and has earned acceptance even in those printing plants continuing to use letterpresses.

New Developments

Anyone who even casually glances through current printing trade magazines knows that not a month goes by without some new development, process or product in the field of lithographic printing making an appearance. Printing supply houses carry an almost bewildering number of offerings, including new surfacing materials for inking rollers, improved dampener rollers and dampener roller covers, better offset blankets, different dampening solutions and many types and grades of offset plates. These products are designed to help the offset press operator overcome or circumvent specific printing problems.

The person who plans to stay abreast the continually changing characteristics of offset lithography will devote considerably more than a cursory examination to these trade periodicals and other readily available sources of information. Every offset press operator should seriously consider acquiring a small personal library of reference material applicable to offset printing in general and to the particular presses and processes currently in use in the plant. In every trade, craft or profession, those who study literature most pertinent to their work tend to advance farthest and fastest. They do better work, receive more compensation, develop greater job satisfaction and individually attain a higher degree of job security.

For background information, the Graphic Arts Technical Foundation remains one of the best sources of books, pamphlets and technical papers that offer in-depth, up-to-date expositions on every phase of offset lithography. Many of these books are available in local libraries or through the inter-library loan service; in this way one can learn whether the information in a particular work would warrant its purchase. Acquaintance with many other books on the theory, history, development and actual practice of offset lithography also can be made in this manner. The operator can decide which of the many published offerings would prove the most helpful addition to a personal collection of source material.

Many printing supply houses also offer literature the operator will find helpful. Much of this literature, though primarily of a promotional or advertising nature, contains extremely valuable and immediately applicable information. Some companies, such as the Minnesota Mining and Manufacturing Company and the Van Son Holland Ink Corp. of America, also make available a wide variety of technical papers, pamphlets and in some cases highly illustrated and detailed instruction manuals or guides 50 to 100 pages in length. Additionally, most printing supply companies maintain staffs of technical advisers to help the operator surmount any printing problem that might arise.

The field of offset lithography expands and changes daily. The offset press operator who hopes to continue to produce high quality work on a competitive basis likewise must expand his or her knowledge of the craft. The operator who not only has grasped the basic theories of lithography but understands a good deal of its history and recent development will be most prepared to meet or even anticipate important changes and technical advances as they occur.

Chapter 1
Preparing the Offset Press

Work of acceptable quality with an offset press, as with any other finely engineered piece of equipment, begins with basic preparation of the machine. So vital is press preparation that many offset technicians consider it an important part of press makeready or pre-makeready. Offset press preparation includes three general areas of activity, none of which the operator can ignore:

1. Lubrication;
2. Cleaning;
3. Adjusting the three basic components of the press — dampening or moistening rollers, inking rollers and printing cylinders.

Lubrication

Before attempting to lubricate an unfamiliar press, study a copy of the operator's manual for the machine. This booklet should provide explicit instructions for proper lubrication; ideally, it will contain a schematic drawing in the form of an exploded view of the press that pinpoints all the oil and grease cups and all the many oil holes around the press. If the booklet does not have such a chart or drawing, it definitely will be advantageous to obtain one from the manufacturer of the press. In addition, the operator's manual should indicate the type of lubricant to use at these various points around the machine.

Study the lubrication chart carefully to avoid missing any point that requires one of the lubricants suggested. Most newer presses have oil holes and cups marked with a spot of paint to indicate the optimum frequency of lubrication. For instance, a red spot on or near an oil hole may mean "oil once each day," while green tells the operator "oil once each week," and a third color indicates a spot requiring less frequent attention. Keep the semiautomatic oiler filled on those presses that have this convenience and activate the mechanism at the recommended intervals.

Generally, it's best to lubricate at the beginning of each shift of work those points requiring daily attention. Lubricate the once-a-week spots on the morning of the first day of the work week. Other points can be lubricated once each month or at the end of a specified number of hours of operation. The important thing here is to set up a lubrication schedule that becomes a matter of routine.

A press run at high speeds for long periods may require a second oiling of the once-a-day areas to avoid friction and undue wear of fast-moving parts. At the very least, stop a heavily used press once in mid-shift and examine these and other critical areas such as main bearings for excessive heat build-up.

A note of caution: Never attempt to lubricate a press while it is in operation. The deceptively simple task of oiling a machine demands the operator's full attention to avoid needless mishaps to the machine or to the worker.

As the operator plies the oiler, he should avoid flooding oil holes with large amounts of oil. This both wastes oil and creates an unnecessary and hazardous accumulation of a highly flammable substance under and around the press. This tends to upset OSHA people and local fire marshals. Wipe away excess oil with a rag before proceeding to the next point. Some press operators oil a few holes, then turn the press over by hand to let the oil drain down through the meshing parts. Continue around the press until all points have received lubrication. If the operator goes around the press in the same direction each time he oils it he is far less likely to miss a spot.

Unless the instruction manual specifies otherwise, use a good grade of No. 20 S.A.E. non-detergent oil for the points lubricated each day. Oil the feeder and delivery drive chains once a week with a light penetrating oil. Apply a good grade of gear grease or similar lubricating compound to the various driving gears on the press, replenishing as frequently as inspection shows a need. Most drive motors need weekly oiling, though grease fittings usually require refilling once every six months or every 1,000 hours of operation. Keep the vacuum pump oiler filled as recommended, usually with a light machine oil.

It's important to apply the correct weight or kind of lubricant to each moving part of the press. If grease or heavy oils are used where the instruction manual recommends lightweight oils, or vice versa, serious operating difficulties will result. A heavy oil or grease may gum up and slow the movement of small parts and cause several kinds of printing problems, including mis-register of the printed material, erratic behavior of the dampening or moistening rollers and poor ink distribution. On the other hand, light oil may drain away too rapidly from heavier parts of the press, quickly subjecting these areas to the high heat and wearing effect of friction.

Though a complete oiling and greasing operation does consume a certain amount of time, an old adage holds as true today as the day it was coined: "It is easier to lubricate than it is to repair." The fact is that more presses wear out from lack of proper lubrication and cleaning than from any other cause. A properly lubricated press runs smoother and quieter as the various parts of the press mesh or move past one another without binding. This plays an important part in achieving good quality printing with a press that will hold up under the pressures of daily operation and give many years of excellent service.

Cleaning the Press

On an offset press, as on a cylinder letterpress, the paper being printed may travel several feet from feeder unit to delivery table. Along the line of travel each sheet comes into momentary contact with many different elements of the press: feeder unit side guides, separating and forwarding suckers, conveyor belts, register guides and head stops, cylinder grippers and, finally, the delivery box or tray and the jogging mechanism.

At any of these points of contact, the sheet may pick up a spot of oil, a smudge of grease or a smear of ink unless the operator keeps the machine perfectly clean. Sometimes such a defect runs undetected from start to finish of a job of printing. Needless to say, this ruins the entire job.

A good way to keep the press clean is to clean it a bit every day. During the oiling operation wipe away obvious collections of grease, dirt and ink. Use a lint-free rag to avoid clogging oiled spindles, gears and bearers with bits of cloth. Keep the rag handy so other parts of the press can be wiped clean during the day. As in oiling the press, never try to clean any part of it while it is in operation. This dangerous practice merely serves to increase the cost of accident insurance and hospital services.

Occasionally, the press will need a thorough cleaning from front to back.

Go over the feeder unit with a rag dampened with a good cleaning solvent. Wipe all the parts dry and clean away any patches of oil or lumps of grease. Clean off the lifting and forwarding suckers and the mechanism that controls them. In tight places such as inside the pullout rollers, use an old toothbrush soaked in solvent to remove clogged dirt or grease.

Conveyor tapes often can be cleaned sufficiently by briskly rubbing them with soapstone or french chalk. This both cleans and dries the tapes and prevents a sticky build-up of ink deposited by previously printed sheets from slowing the progress of the running sheets on the second printing or smudging their reverse sides. As the tapes are cleaned, examine and wipe the various hold-down straps and bars that serve to keep the sheets flat on the tapes. Dirt or ink clinging to the underside of these parts frequently mars the running sheets on their way to the printing cylinder.

Turn the press over by hand until the grippers on the impression cylinder come into view in the open position and can be cleaned. Clean the activating mechanism of these grippers as well. Wipe the chain delivery grippers, the chain delivery, the delivery jogger and any part in the delivery that might come in contact with the printed sheet.

Dirt can come from many odd sources on an offset press. Dust or excessive oil in the area of the vacuum pump can lead to a spray of dirty air being forced through the air blowers onto the sheets in the feeder. Contaminated anti-setoff spray, especially infrequently used cornstarch, can result in dirtied sheets in the delivery stack. Oily dirt or chips of dried ink knocked from the wire delivery cover found on some machines will ruin the sheets below. A film of dried anti-setoff spray allowed to remain caked on the sides of the delivery box or on the delivery box guides can break loose at inconvenient moments and ruin several sheets. Sticking rubber-covered pullout rollers may leave a black mark on every sheet or at irregular intervals throughout the press run, even though the rollers have been wiped clean of oil and dirt.

In addition to actual contamination of the printed material, dirt, gum, oil or dried ink can cause other printing difficulties. Oil or grease will distort rubber lifting or forwarding suckers and lead to porosity of the material. A coating of dried ink on the suckers interferes with the suction and eventually will cause the rubber to crack. If one of the pullout rollers becomes clogged with dirt it may hold back one side of the sheet and cause the sheet to feed crookedly into the register guides. If one of the grippers fails to close properly because of impacted dirt, either a mis-register or a tearing of the sheet may occur.

The moments devoted to cleaning an offset press cannot be considered wasted time. Cleaning the press, like oiling it, supplements all the other efforts taken to produce good quality work. It is an element of press preparation the operator cannot afford to overlook.

Adjusting the Press

Precise settings of the ink fountain and the dampener fountain and especially of the inking and dampening rollers provide the operator with an important line of defense against several printing problems that can follow a breakdown of the ink/water balance. Correct setting of the three printing cylinders—the plate, the blanket and the impression cylinders—prove equally vital to the achievement of good quality work on the offset press.

More explicit instructions on the various adjustments and settings of these segments of the offset press appear in Chapter 6. Some of these parts of the press are factory-set and need little or no adjusting. Others require adjustment by the operator. The material that follows is designed primarily to alert the operator to those areas of the press that need periodic examination and occasional pre-makeready adjustment to bring them into precise contact or proper alignment with other parts of the press.

First, the inking rollers. During operation of the press the bank or chain of inking rollers performs two separate functions. 1.

It picks up ink from the ink fountain roller and distributes it in a thin, even film across the surface of all the rollers. 2. It applys this film of ink to the image areas of the offset plate. In order for the rollers to perform these functions properly they must be correctly set.

The ductor roller swings back and forth with a metronomic action to pick up ink from the ink fountain roller and transfer it to the first of the distributing rollers. Be sure the ductor roller strikes both the fountain and the distributor roller squarely. Otherwise it will not transfer the ink evenly. Be equally certain that the various distributing and vibrator rollers that make up the distributing section of the inking system turn in perfectly parallel contact with each other.

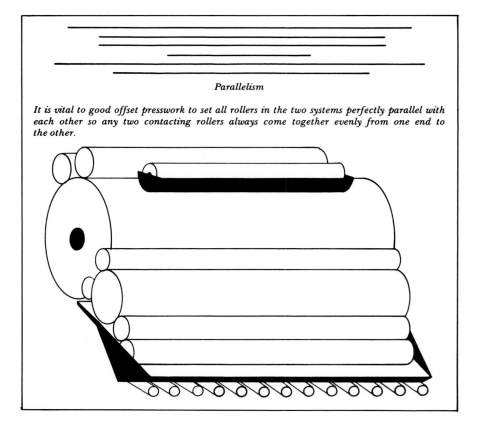

Parallelism

It is vital to good offset presswork to set all rollers in the two systems perfectly parallel with each other so any two contacting rollers always come together evenly from one end to the other.

The rollers most likely to get out of perfect adjustment are those rollers that most need to stay in adjustment, the form rollers. These larger rubber or composition rollers have the critical function of transferring ink from the distributing rollers to the turning plate in a thin, even film. To do this properly, they must contact the plate squarely and with the correct pressure. If the form rollers contact the plate unevenly or bang heavily against it, the transferred film of ink will be uneven or ruptured. Excessive plate wear also may occur. The form rollers also must be free from serious end play or they may skid laterally over the plate's surface and smear or rupture the ink film.

An important part of press preparation, then, involves setting the inking rollers. Set them square and set them with the proper pressures. This insures an even flow of ink throughout the inking system and results in a thin, even film of color on the plate.

The dampener rollers are fewer in number than the inking rollers on an offset press. Nevertheless, it is important that the fountain roller, the ductor roller, the vibrator roller or rollers and the form dampening roller or rollers be set properly. Set the rollers parallel with one another so a full charge of fountain solution transfers from roller to roller across the entire length of each roller in the system. If the ductor roller fails to contact the fountain roller squarely, it cannot possibly pick up a full, even charge of the solution and transfer it to the next roller in line. As a consequence, the form dampening roller will provide inadequate amounts of moisture for one side of the plate.

Be sure the dampener rollers are set with correct pressures. Too much or too little, improper pressures usually result in a lowering of the quality of the printing. This especially is so in the case of the form dampening rollers that must maintain that all-important ink/water balance on the plate's surface. Excessive form dampening roller pressures also may seriously damage the printing image and thus shorten the life of the plate.

Once the inking and dampening rollers have produced the desired ink/water balance and properly inked and dampened the plate, the action of the three printing cylinders comes into play. Two cylinder adjustments most concern the offset press operator: plate-to-blanket and blanket-to-impression cylinder pressures.

Unless proper adjustments are obtained at the two points where these three cylinders meet either insufficient or excessive or uneven pressures will result in a poor transfer of the inked image from plate to blanket to paper.

The first step, determining the correctness of plate-to-blanket pressure, involves examining the width of an ink band carefully pressed onto a clean blanket from a fully inked, blank offset plate. The band should measure from 1/8″ to 3/16″ wide on most presses. If the band's width falls outside the rather narrow limits specified in the operator's manual, adjust the plate-to-blanket cylinder pressure by bringing the cylinders closer together or moving them further apart, following the instructions in the manual. Remember that on those offset presses requiring underpacking, the number of packing sheets placed under the plate or the blanket can affect this pressure.

On some offset presses, the impression cylinder adjusts "automatically" to accommodate different weights of paper. Even with these presses, however, a coarse-finished paper may require careful manual adjustment of the impression cylinder to obtain a sharp, clear reproduction of the image. In adjusting the impression cylinder pressure, first back off the pressure then bring the cylinder into gradually heavier contact with the blanket cylinder to get the sharpest image possible on the printed sheets. Avoid excessive pressure. This eventually ruins the blanket. On some presses the impression cylinder can be leveled, or set square with the blanket cylinder by increasing or decreasing the pressure on one side of the cylinder only.

None of the operations outlined on these pages, including the critical roller and cylinder settings and adjustments, should prove beyond the capabilities of anyone willing to study the press operator's manual and follow the detailed instructions given there while proceeding systematically and with the caution due expensive equipment. The operator cannot escape the results of failing to lubricate, clean and maintain the press in proper adjustment. On the other hand, the operator who conscientiously performs the necessary tasks of press preparation will more consistently produce work of professional quality on the offset press.

Chapter 2
The Offset Plate

The photochemical image used in offset printing requires a thin, flexible carrier easily secured to a cylindrical surface. We call the image carrier the offset plate. Manufacturers today make several types of offset plates: paper plates, metal plates, plastic plates, plastic-and-metal plates, and certain bi-metal plates. The offset plates most commonly used are metal plates and paper plates. Many refer to the paper plates as 'paper masters.'

Handling the Plate

Offset plates have an extremely high susceptibility to damage from careless handling. This is especially true of paper plates, which bend, wrinkle or tear easily. Allowing a paper plate to lie in a pool of water or cleaning solvent will ruin it. Metal plates, though more durable and generally physically impervious to moisture, also require care in handling.

In preparing an offset plate for the press, work on a clean, dry, smooth surface. Many press operators keep near at hand several clean sheets of a fairly thick, porous paper and place one or more of these on the work table. This provides a smooth working surface for sponging down the plates, and the paper absorbs any excess moisture.

When working on a bare surface, wipe it clean before laying a new plate on it. Bits of dirt or metal that become imbedded in the back side of a plate will create small, pimple-like defects on the image side of the plate. Usually, these small defects on a metal plate can be corrected without too much difficulty, but hard particles of foreign matter can punch holes right through a paper plate and ruin it beyond repair.

Learn to lift an offset plate by two diagonally opposite corners, with the image facing up. This imparts a natural roll or curve in a plate and prevents the formation of a crease or wrinkle in the thin material. The image surface of the plate inside the roll remains protected from scratches while the plate is moved from one work area to another.

Despite every precaution, a metal plate may acquire a crease or a kink during handling. A small crease usually flattens out when the plate clamps draw the plate tight around the plate cylinder. If not, lay a piece of blotter paper over the crease and tap it lightly with a rubber mallet. If this fails to smooth out the crease, remove the plate from the press and sandwich it between protective sheets of paper. Lay it image side down on the work table and flatten the crease with a small rubber roller worked back and forth over the plate with considerable pressure.

While checking the plate for physical defects, examine the image on the plate for any errors made in processing the plate. It's a waste of time, effort and materials to proceed further if the plate has obvious mistakes. Compare the image with the original copy or dummy to be sure all elements of the layout appear on the plate, in the proper order and specified arrangement. Check register marks and centermarks on those plates paired for color or other register work to be sure these match. Be sure that no scratches, holes or breaks mar the halftone areas of the image. The press operator usually can repair a scratch in the solid area of the image. Other processing errors probably will require returning the plate to the platemaking department for correction or replacement.

If the plate cylinder of the press requires sheets of underpacking, do not secure the plate to the cylinder without ascertaining the correct underpacking for the particular plate in use. Most offset press technicians proceed as follows to determine the number of packing sheets to place under a plate:

First, discover the "under-cut" of the plate cylinder. This is the distance between the bare cylinder surface and the plane of the two cylinder bearers, which will appear to be a few thousandths of an inch higher than the cylinder surface. Look for this information stamped in the gutter next to one of the cylinder bearers or printed on the specification chart for the press; if not, write the press manufacturer and obtain it at once. Many operators refer to the undercut as the bearer height. Either designation is correct.

Second, discover the thickness of the plate. Do not depend entirely upon the plate manufacturer to supply this information. Use a micrometer and measure the actual thickness of the plate you plan to install. Plate thicknesses vary according to their type and manufacturer. All the plates from a single package should possess the same thickness and require identical amounts of underpacking; but if a fading image indicates a sudden loss of impression, remove the plate from the press and measure it's thickness to be sure.

The thickness of the plate, when added to the thickness of the packing sheets, should equal the undercut. *

'Miking' the Plate

On those offset presses that require sheets of underpacking under the plate, obtaining accurate impression pressures often requires the operator to measure the thickness of the plate and the packing sheets.

Some technicians recommend an initial overpacking of the plate cylinder to .001" above bearer height to compensate for any compression of the packing sheets during printing. On multicolor jobs requiring close register of the printed images, slightly overpacking the plate cylinder and underpacking the blanket cylinder an equal amount allows for a subsequent adjustment of the packing on second or third printings to compensate for any moisture stretch of the printed sheets.

Example:

Undercut	.010"
Less Thickness of the Plate	.004"
Underpacking Required	.006"

Keep a supply of pre-calipered and pre-cut packing sheets near the press—in thicknesses of .001", .002", .003", .004" and .007". This eases the task of packing the plate cylinder; the operator need only measure the plate's thickness, then add sheets of different calipers accordingly. Use the least number of sheets possible to bring the plate to bearer height. Use hard, stiff paper for underpacking sheets. They handle easier, and tend to trap less air than soft, flimsy sheets. Keep the different calipers of paper on separate storage shelves or sandwich them between sheets of labeled cardboard.

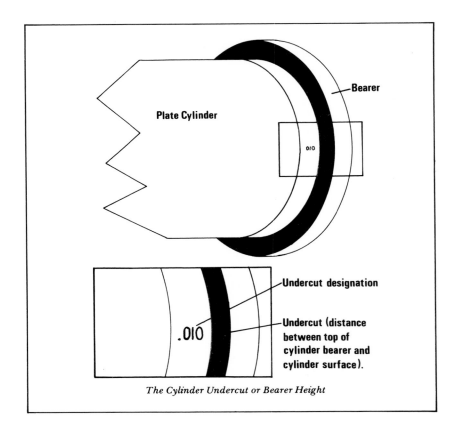

The Cylinder Undercut or Bearer Height

Though many operators pre-moisten a plate after mounting it on the press, some feel it's best to perform this operation on the work table just prior to securing the plate to the plate cylinder. With the plate lying on a flat surface you are less likely to miss any portion of it with the moistening sponge. In any case, pre-moisten the plate according to the manufacturer's recommendations. Or, pre-moisten metal plates with a diluted fountain solution at the rate of 15 ounces of water to 1 ounce of mixed fountain solution and pre-moisten paper plates with undiluted fountain solution.

Before mounting the plate, go over the plate cylinder with a rag and wipe it clean and dry. Any moisture trapped under a paper plate will cause wrinkles or creases in the plate and lead to rapid deterioration of the image. A small bit of metal or a lump of dried ink between the cylinder surface and a plate easily can ruin the plate after a few impressions. Examine the back of the plate itself again to be sure no hard foreign matter adheres to it.

Mounting the Plate

The basic steps for mounting a plate on an offset press are as follows:

1. Turn the press over by hand to bring the leading edge of the plate cylinder into working position.

2. When using a slotted plate, fit the slots of the leading edge of the plate onto the engaging pins of the plate cylinder. Hold the trailing edge of the plate firmly with your right hand and fit the leading edge of the plate squarely into position with your left hand. Straight-edged (unslotted) plates are designed for presses with clamps or clamping bars. Be sure the clamping bar sets parallel to the edge of the cylinder before inserting the plate. Open the clamp and insert the leading edge of the plate, squarely seating it all the way into the clamp; tighten the clamp securely onto the plate.

3. Insert the packing sheets, if any, as far under the leading edge of the plate as possible.

4. Hold the plate by its trailing edge to keep it aligned with the cylinder and turn the press over by hand until the trailing edge of the cylinder comes into working position. On larger presses, put the plate and blanket cylinders on impression and use the jogging button to inch the cylinder into position. Impression pressures help smooth out the plate and the packing sheets under it. Whether

inching the machine around or turning it over by hand, work carefully to avoid wrinkling either the plate or any of the packing sheets.

Any difficulty in securing the plate to the rear clamping device often can be overcome simply by applying dampener-to-plate pressure while turning or jogging the cylinder forward. The dampener roller or rollers will prevent any side-to-side movement of the plate until it has been secured by the rear clamps.

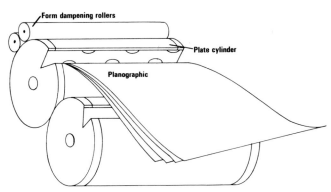

A. Secure plate and underpacking sheets (if required) to forward clamping device, then turn the press forward while keeping the plate smoothed to the plate cylinder surface.

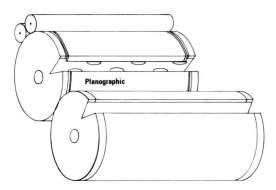

B. When rear clamping device rises into working position secure the tail end of the plate snugly into place, watching for wrinkles or serious sideways displacement of the plate.

5. When the rear engaging pins or clamping bar rise into position, secure the trailing edge of the plate in place. If the rear clamping bar or plate-holding device has tension knobs, draw these up evenly. Follow the instructions in the operator's manual, or work from one to another, tightening each tension knob a little at a time with thumb and forefinger, then finish tightening them by giving them a 1/4 to 1/2 turn with a pin wrench. Avoid overtensioning the plates, especially paper plates which tear easily under excessive pressure. Usually, paper plates require only the amount of tension provided by the clamping device spring to keep them pulled taut against the cylinder surface. Over-tension also can cause an aluminum plate to tear during operation of the press and may stretch a zinc plate severely enough to affect the register of the image.

To remove a plate from the press, merely reverse the steps of installation. Release the rear clamping device and turn the press backward with one hand while pulling on the trailing edge of the plate with the other hand. When the lead clamping device rises into position, release the leading edge of the plate and remove it from the cylinder.

Adjusting the Plate

Not infrequently, the printing image appears slightly tilted on the plate. Depending on the press, the operator can use one of two methods to correct the image angle. One method involves adjusting the plate on the cylinder. The other method simply requires angling the paper as it feeds into the register guides.

On the ATF (American Type Founders) Chief, for instance, correcting the angle of the printed image calls for a simple adjustment made to the paper stop bar at the forward end of the conveyor or feed table. An adjusting screw allows the paper stop bar to be tilted in either direction. The angled stop bar positions each sheet at a corrected angle as it enters the printing cylinders so the image appears square when printed on the sheet.

On presses not equipped with a paper angling device, correcting the image angle proves somewhat more complicated. Correcting the image angle on these presses requires angling the plate on the plate cylinder. A lateral adjustment device located at the leading edge of the cylinder moves the leading edge of the plate to the right or to the left on the cylinder. A similar device at the rear edge of the cylinder moves the trailing edge of the plate to the right or left.

The proper procedure for large adjustments of the image is to move the forward and rear edges of the plate laterally in opposite directions on the cylinder. Otherwise a twist in the plate might wrinkle or tear it. Move each lateral adjustment device just half the distance required to square the image on the paper. Minor adjustments to correct the image angle often require only moving the trailing edge of the plate to the right or left with the rear lateral adjustment device.

To move the top of the image to the right on the printed sheet, move the top of the plate to the right and the bottom of the plate to the left or move the top of the sheet to the left and the bottom of the sheet to the right.

Many operators simplify this operation by lightly penciling guidelines on the plate horizontal to the image and lining up these lines with positioning marks scribed on each side of the plate cylinder. These positioning marks, scribed on the bearers or on the cylinder, should represent the point at which printing begins with the cylinders at normal settings. This distance may vary from press to press. If necessary, write the press manufacturer and ascertain the minimum distance between the leading edge of the plate and the point at which printing can begin. Some press manufacturers have lines representing this distance already scribed on the plate cylinder. If the machine in use lacks positioning marks, use a sharp metal stylus or the corner of a small file to scratch a very fine positioning mark on either side of the plate cylinder. These guides are an invaluable aid. It is only necessary to align the image with these scribed marks when positioning the plate to be sure the image lies parallel to the plate cylinder's edge.

In penciling guide lines on the plate, place a short line (A) at one side of the plate the specified distance back from the gripper edge of the plate at which printing can begin. Now measure the distance between A and the top of the image on the plate or between A and any horizontal line of copy within the image. Call this distance C. On the opposite side of the plate measure this distance

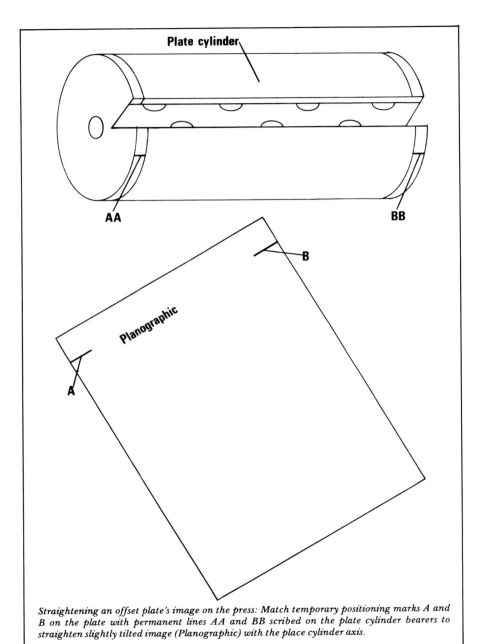

Straightening an offset plate's image on the press: Match temporary positioning marks A and B on the plate with permanent lines AA and BB scribed on the plate cylinder bearers to straighten slightly tilted image (Planographic) with the place cylinder axis.

(*C*) from the top of the image (or the horizontal line of copy) back toward the leading edge of the plate. Pencil another short line (*B*) here.

If the image lies at an angle on the plate, an imaginary line drawn between *A* and *B* will not run parallel to the edge of the plate. It will, however, run parallel to the image. To align the image with the printing cylinders, place the penciled lines (*A* and *B*) on either side of the plate directly opposite the positioning marks scribed on the plate cylinder or cylinder bearers. With the image and the imaginary line between *A* and *B* thus lying parallel to the edge of the plate cylinder, merely bring the lead plate clamping device into alignment with the plate before inserting the plate.

Adjusting the image horizontally usually is done by moving the conveyor table side guide and jogger mechanisms to the right or the left the desired distance. With the image correctly centered on the sheet, reposition the stack of paper in the feeder unit accordingly. On presses having lateral adjustment devices, the operator occasionally may find it more convenient to move the image the desired distance horizontally by moving both the lead and rear lateral adjustment devices to the right or left an equal amount.

It is possible on most presses to adjust the image position vertically in relation to the top of the registered sheet entering the printing cylinders. This adjustment involves moving the plate cylinder or the blanket cylinder, or both, forward or backward the desired amount, independent of other parts of the machine. Make the vertical positioning adjustment after pulling an impression to determine how far the image should be moved toward the top or toward the bottom of the sheet.

A vertical control knob, usually located at one side of the press opposite the outer edge of one of the cylinders, releases the cylinder locking nut. Rotate the cylinder by hand until the control knob is aligned with the locking nut and unlock the cylinder. Now turn the handwheel until the image (plate cylinder) moves forward or backward the desired distance. A numbered positioning scale at the outside edge of the cylinder permits accurate positioning of the image.

This important adjustment works differently on each make of press. Not all are as complicated as the above might indicate. On one small offset press, for instance, the vertical position control knob or wheel is located in the gap of the plate cylinder; the image is raised and lowered simply by turning the wheel counterclockwise or clockwise. Carefully study the operator's manual for the press until the specific instructions concerning vertical positioning of the image are understood. It is an adjustment that will be made again and again.

With the plate correctly positioned on the cylinder and locked both front and back, check it for any slack. To do this, disengage the ink form rollers and the form dampening rollers and put the press on impression. Run the press at slow speed five or ten revolutions, observing the plate. Stop the press and examine the plate for any looseness.

With the plate secured perfectly flat and smooth to the cylinder surface, with lateral, horizontal and vertical adjustments made as required, the plate should be ready for operation of the press.

Chapter 3
The Inking System
and Ink

The pasty substance we call ink almost defies definition. To call it a dispersion or suspension of coloring pigment particles in a fluid medium comes the nearest to presenting a one-line description. However, not all inks contain pigment as the coloring substance; dye-colored inks find many uses in the printing industry. Nor do all inks come in liquid form. Cold-set inks, designed to dry or harden when cooled, remain solid at room temperatures; they must be heated to a liquid paste before and during use.

Nevertheless, most inks used in offset printing are liquid or fluid in nature and do contain coloring pigment particles of different hues and strengths. The finely ground pigment particles remain suspended in a liquid or paste-like medium called the vehicle. The vehicle, or carrier, flows through the inking system in a thin film, carrying with it the pigment particles. The ink form rollers distribute vehicle and coloring matter evenly across the plate, which transfers an inked image to the offset blanket. From here the image transfers again to the surface of the material being printed.

Because of the wide variety of printing surfaces, the different circumstances under which printing occurs and the seemingly endless number of end-use requirements of the printed material, the vehicle normally carries one or more ingredients other than, but just as vital as, the coloring matter. These include binders, driers, waxes, varnishes, oils and anti-skinning compounds, to name just a few. Too much of an ingredient or additive can cause printing difficulties as easily as too little.

Anyone unfamiliar with offset printing processes should begin by ordering inks specially formulated for the printing immediately planned or contemplated in the near future. This is especially so in the case of unusual printing surfaces. Press-ready inks designed for decalcomania (decal) printing, foil printing, label printing, metal decorating and for plastic surfaces should require little or no prepress preparation. Purchase good grades of ink from a reliable manufacturer to avoid unnecessary problems with special or unfamiliar printing surfaces. The manufacturer has equipment to test different vehicles, pigments, waxes, varnishes and binders on any printing surface and can produce an ink formula best suited for that surface.

Altering Lithographic Inks and Mixing Colors

Sooner or later, of course, the operator will find it necessary to add some compound or ingredient to an ink to increase its distributing, covering, absorption or drying efficiency. Usually, an ink will require only a small amount of an additive to alter it sufficiently. It must be remembered that anything added to an ink will reduce its color strength to a certain extent. Consequently, add no more than the minimum amount of any compound necessary to perform the required task.

A varnish of greater or lesser viscosity than the ink will alter the ink's flowing qualities when added to it. A more viscous varnish tends to stiffen the ink, while a less viscous varnish increases the ink's flowability. The viscosity of lithographic varnishes ranges from No. 00000 (very thin) through No. 1 or No. 0 (medium) to No. 9 or No. 10 (quite thick or sticky). An ink's tack or stickiness also varies with its viscosity. Tack, the characteristic which permits the ink to cling fast to the surface being printed, increases as the ink's viscosity increases.

Driers, when added to inks in small amounts, promote oxidation and hasten drying of the printing ink film. Driers in use today contain one or more of the following: cobalt, calcium, copper, iron, lead, manganese, zinc and zirconium. These substances usually come from the supplier dispersed in a medium-thin varnish for ease of mixture into the ink. Partly because other substances have proved either less effective or considerably more toxic to humans, cobalt remains the most popular drier. An ink may require slightly more drier on humid days than on dry days. Too much drier may cause the ink to dry on the rollers and in the ink fountain during operation of the press.

Cornstarch may help prevent setoff of the printed ink film when added to the ink. The large cornstarch particles in the ink prevent sheets from coming into close contact until the ink has had time to set or dry. But add cornstarch to offset inks cautiously. The large particles may fill in a fine halftone screen.

A binding varnish mixed into an ink will add body to it and improve its ability to adhere to certain surfaces. Also it will increase the ink's ability to resist admixture with water, preventing both water-in-ink emulsion and ink-in-water emulsion. This latter problem leads to bleeding of random pigment particles into the dampening solution and causes a tint of the ink to appear in the non-image areas of the printed material.

These and other substances such as waxes, oils, ground pigment, and anti-skinning compounds, will be used by the offset press operator from time to time in order to condition various inks to meet different printing circumstances. Be sure to mix in the additive thoroughly to distribute it evenly throughout the ink.

Another task that not infrequently faces the operator of single-color presses involves mixing together inks of two or more colors in order to match a shade or hue to satisfy the requirements of a particular job of printing.* In mixing inks, use inks of identical or similar properties from the same manufacturer. Mixing together two inks having different drying characteristics, absorption rates or inks that contain incompatible ingredients can spoil both inks.

Mix up a small test batch of the ink at first, thoroughly mixing small portions of the darker ink into comparatively larger portions of the light ink until you have a match of the desired color. Note the amount used of each ink. Test the match by pulling a thin drawdown of your mixture on a sample of the paper you plan to use. If the drawdown matches the sample satisfactorily, proceed to mix up enough ink for the job of printing.

Handle all offset inks with care. Store opened and unopened cans at normal room temperatures in a clean, well-lighted area.

---

*The economics of printing with large, high-speed multicolor offset presses usually require the purchase of inks ready mixed in the colors needed for different jobs printed on these more sophisticated presses.

Remove ink from the cans carefully, taking pains to discard every bit of dried ink on the surface and around the edges of the can. Small dried-ink particles admitted to the ink system quickly give rise to hickies in the printed image and require a thorough cleaning of the inking system from ink fountain to form rollers.

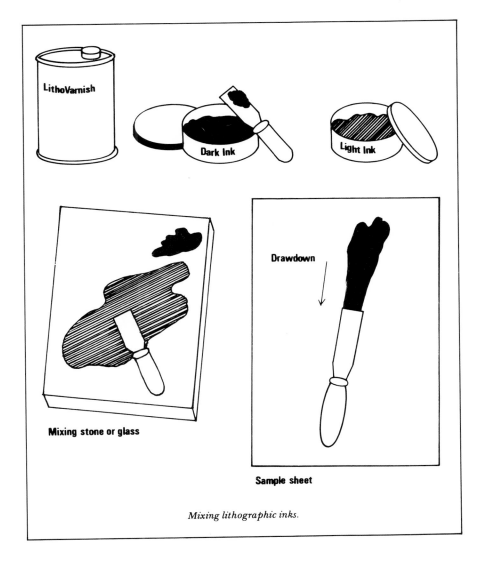

Mixing lithographic inks.

The Inking Rollers

In addition to using inks properly formulated for the printing surface and designed to meet particular press, drying and end-use requirements, the operator must make sure the inking system correctly performs the task of distributing the ink in a thin film across the rollers and applying it evenly to the image areas of the plate. This calls for an understanding of how the offset press inking system works and of the various adjustments it is necessary for the operator to make to insure continued operating efficiency.

The operator places the ink in a long, shallow receptacle at the rear of the system called the ink fountain. A metal roller that turns intermittently while in constant contact with the ink in the fountain picks up an initial, fairly heavy film of ink from the supply. A small, rubber ductor roller having a rhythmic, metronomic action receives a relatively thick band of ink from the fountain roller and transfers this ink to the next roller in the chain, usually an oscillating metal vibrator roller. A series of intermediate rubber and metal rollers rapidly draws the band or bead of ink into a thin, even film. These rollers also break down the ink into a working consistency as they carry it forward through the inking system. The number of these intermediate distributor rollers varies with the make and size of the press. Finally two form inking rollers apply the film of ink to the image areas of the offset plate.

The action of the form rollers as the plate travels under them must be such that the film of ink is rolled onto the plate's surface, not rubbed, banged or squashed on. To achieve this the rollers must be set to bear against the plate with a correct and constant pressure. This pressure must be even across the entire length of the rollers. Check the pressure between the ink form rollers and the plate in the following manner:

Install a press plate of normal thickness and pack it to cylinder bearer height. Run the press with the inking system "on," but with the ink form rollers lifted, until all the rollers have acquired a normal film of ink. Switch off the power and turn the press over by hand until the plate lies directly under the ink form rollers. Gently lower both form rollers into contact with the plate. Let the rollers rest in contact with the plate for the count of four or five, then raise them and turn the press by hand until the plate moves into position to permit a visual inspection of the two thin lines or bands of ink.

On a small press these ink bands should be uniformly 1/8"
wide from end to end. On larger presses the instruction manual
may recommend slightly wider bands. This depends on the
diameter of the ink form rollers. Rollers having a diameter up to
2½ inches should produce a test band from 1/8" to 3/16" wide.
Rollers larger than 2½ inches in diameter should produce a band
from 1/4" to 5/16" wide on the plate. An examination of the bands
placed on the plate tells the discerning eye quite a bit about form
roller condition as well as roller pressure settings.

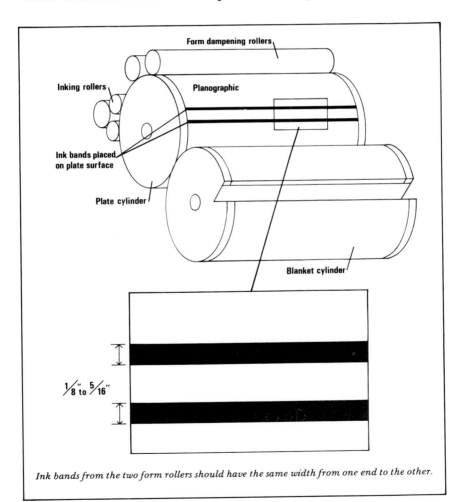

Ink bands from the two form rollers should have the same width from one end to the other.

Even band indicates ideal roller pressure setting.

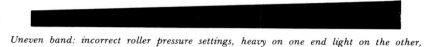

Uneven band: incorrect roller pressure settings, heavy on one end light on the other, or worn roller.

Fat-centered band indicating a roller with badly worn ends: excessive vibrator-to-form roller pressure.

Band narrow in center areas indicates an inking roller with swollen ends: excessive form roller-to-plate pressure.

Band having narrow area(s) toward the center indicates a roller improperly ground at the factory.

A band that's wider or narrower than the recommended width indicates too much or too little pressure exists between the roller that created it and the plate. A band narrow on one end and wide on the other indicates uneven pressure, with one end of the roller striking the plate harder than the other. If the band has a fat middle, that is, appears wider in the middle than it does at both ends, the roller that made it likely has excessively worn ends. Too much pressure between the form roller and the adjacent oscillating rider roller usually is responsible for this condition, which often requires replacement of the roller. An ink band that's markedly narrower through the middle and wide at the very ends indicates excessive form roller-to-plate pressure. A band narrowing abruptly toward the center may indicate a roller improperly ground at the factory. Here again, obtaining a good ink transfer from roller to plate surface may require roller replacement.

From the foregoing, one can see the importance of maintaining correct roller pressures at all times.

Setting Roller Pressures

Ink form roller pressure settings are made differently on different makes of presses. Commonly, the lock nut or screw and the adjusting screw that control a roller's pressure settings are located outside the press frame at one end of the roller. But on some presses these will be found inside the press frame, in the form roller brackets. The lock nut, lock screw or set screw is first loosened to free the adjacent pressure adjusting screw. Turn the adjusting screw clockwise or counterclockwise to decrease or increase the width of the ink band.

In adjusting form roller pressure settings the operator must refer to the instruction manual for the machine in use and follow the directions carefully.

Adjust roller pressures until both bands on the plate appear uniformly wide from end to end. Check the bands after each change of the settings until the correct pressure has been attained.

Some offset press operators set form roller pressures in a different manner. They set the roller that first contacts the plate with slightly more pressure than the second ink form roller. They feel better results follow when the first form roller applies an initial, relatively heavy charge of ink to the plate while the next roller, set with lighter pressure to the plate, acts as a clean-up roller, clearing the plate of ink scum and otherwise sharpening the image. The utility of this practice for all makes of presses is debatable. The individual press operator must experiment with roller pressure settings and decide whether or not this method improves ink distribution and image reproduction on the machine in use.

Since the pressure between the vibrator rollers and the form rollers they contact can affect form roller settings as well as control distribution of the ink to the form rollers, the operator should set these rider rollers at the same time the form rollers are set. A reliable check of vibrator-to-form roller pressures can be made with strips of paper without washing up the press.

Cut two strips of 20-lb. paper 1 inch wide and four strips of tissue paper 1½ inches wide. Sandwich each 20-lb. strip between two wider strips of tissue paper. Insert the ends of these two sets of paper between the form roller and the vibrator roller to be tested, working them well in between the rollers by turning the press over

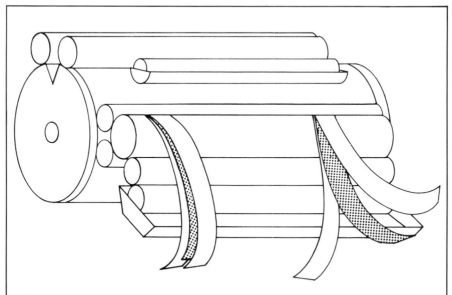

Use strips of paper as illustrated to check the pressure between form inking rollers and the vibrator roller or rollers. Strips of 20-lb. paper sandwiched between tissue strips should have the same drag or pull when withdrawn.

an inch or two by hand. Now pull on the strips of 20-lb. paper. An identical pull or tension should be felt on both strips as they are withdrawn from between the strips of tissue paper. Uneven drag or pull on either side indicates uneven roller pressure. Excessive drag that makes withdrawing both strips of 20-lb. paper impossible or difficult indicates too much overall pressure between the two rollers.

Refer to the instruction manual to determine if the vibrator roller or the form roller is adjusted to change the pressure between them. It will pay to recheck form roller-to-plate pressure settings again once vibrator-to-form roller pressure settings have been corrected. Plate, form roller and vibrator roller pressure settings should be such that the form rollers are driven by the vibrator rollers, not by the revolving plate cylinder.

A check of the pressures between the ductor roller and the fountain roller and the ductor roller and the first distributing roller also can be made with strips of 20-lb. paper sandwiched between strips of tissue paper. Normally, a spring connected to the ductor roller operating mechanism controls the pressure between the ductor roller and the fountain roller or between the ductor roller and the distributing roller. This leaves but one pressure setting to check. The contact between the ductor roller and the other two rollers should be equally heavy from one end of the rollers to the other. This small but important roller is responsible for feeding ink initially into the inking system. If it has worn areas or fails to make even contact with the other rollers, ink distribution suffers at the outset. Follow the instruction manual for the machine in use to set the ductor roller pressure.

Offset press technicians consider maintaining correct ink form roller pressures most important. Form rollers set too heavily to the plate not only fail to lay an even film of ink over the entire image area, the excessive pressure causes undue wear to the image and results in a shortened plate life. Inadequate pressure fails to place enough ink on the image area and results in unsatisfactory reproduction of the image. The operator, of course, cannot safely ignore pressure settings for any of the rollers in the system. Faulty ink distribution and excessive roller wear follows improper pressure settings of any of the rollers in the inking system.

The Ink Fountain

The ink fountain and ink fountain blade combine to perform an important and vital function by providing an even flow of ink to the inking system. Only by correctly adjusting the control devices on the fountain unit can the operator satisfactorily maintain this flow of ink.

On most presses a lever controlling the ductor roller action determines whether or not the ductor roller moves back and forth to pick up ink from the fountain roller and transfer it to the first distributing roller. Another lever determines how far the fountain roller moves through the supply of ink in the fountain during each revolution of the roller; the further the fountain roller turns through the ink supply the more fresh ink it picks up to present to the metronomic ductor roller. At the lowest setting of this lever, the fountain roller should not turn at all. Be sure that these controlling levers work freely and that they drop snugly into the different notches and remain there until the setting is changed.

A row of adjusting screws or knobs located directly under the fountain regulates the pressure exerted against the turning fountain roller by the metal blade that forms the bottom of the ink fountain. Turning these screws clockwise presses the blade tighter against the roller. This decreases the amount of ink the fountain roller can pull from the ink supply. Releasing the pressure on the blade by turning the screws outward increases the flow of ink.

To prevent warping the ink fountain blade always start with the center screws and work outward toward the ends of the fountain to adjust the ink flow. Adjust each screw a small amount at a time, then move to the next screw and turn it in or out. Avoid turning any of the screws in so tightly that the blade binds against the fountain roller.

In general, best startup results follow when a light flow of ink is admitted to the fountain roller, which is placed in the low-to-medium range settings.

Chapter 4
Dampening Systems and
Dampening Solutions

Most offset presses in use today have a dampening or fountain solution system that duplicates the inking system in several particulars. The dampening system includes a fountain or tray to hold the prepared dampening solution and it has a fountain roller. Next in line is a ductor roller of metronomic action. An oscillating vibrator roller rests or rides on the form dampening roller which contacts the turning offset plate once each revolution of the press. To increase the dampening system's moisture carrying capacity, many presses have more than one form dampening roller.

There are exceptions to this arrangement of rollers. On the A.B. Dick 350/360 models, compact presses designed for quick startups and ease of reproduction of short-run interoffice and business forms, for instance, the dampening system has but two rollers—a fountain roller and a ductor roller. The ductor roller takes moisture from the fountain roller and applies it directly to an inked roller, one of the chain of rollers in the inking system. This roller turns in contact with the first ink form roller. The double charge of ink and dampening solution then distributes over the surface of the plate, usually a paper plate.

The offset press dampening system *differs* from the inking system in two ways. Instead of rubber or composition rollers, the dampening system utilizes cloth- or paper-covered ductor and form rollers. And instead of ink, of course, the dampening system fountain is filled with a chemical solution the greater part of which is water. The fibers in cloth or paper absorb, hold and release moisture in controllable amounts. Offset press operators frequently call the dampening or fountain solution "the water" and though this technically is incorrect, the short-hand term is satisfactorily descriptive for most purposes.

The actual operation of most dampening systems imitates that of the inking system. The fountain roller sets in the fountain tray and turns in constant contact with the supply of fountain solution. A lever controls the distance the fountain roller turns through the solution. This determines the amount of moisture picked up by the roller. The further the roller turns through the supply, at higher notched settings of the lever, the more dampening solution the roller picks up.

During operation of the press the operator should favor the lowest setting possible that provides moisture in amounts sufficient to keep the non-image areas of the plate free from ink.

The metronomic ductor roller alternately contacts the fountain roller and the oscillating vibrator or distributing roller, drawing the film of water into the dampening system. The lateral movement of the oscillating vibrator roller serves to distribute the fountain solution evenly across the full length of the form dampening roller. The form dampening roller contacts the plate just prior to the ink form rollers and covers the non-image areas of the plate with a film of ink-repelling fountain solution.

Depending on the make of the press, a lever, knob or small handle on the operator's side of the machine raises the form dampening roller into idling position and lowers it into contact with the plate during operation of the press. Since the press operator commences each press run by first lowering the form dampening roller and then the ink form roller or rollers, he must quickly develop a working familiarity with the location and sequence of operation of these important controls on the press.

Pay particular attention to the action or feel of these levers when they are working normally. Be sure you can turn them into a full "on" or full "off" position quickly. Nothing should hinder their movement. Anything that prevents full on or full off of either the inking or the dampening rollers obviously will cause printing difficulties.

The start-up operation differs slightly on the A.B. Dick machines where all ink rollers are thoroughly inked before any prepared fountain solution is added to the fountain and where proper operating sequence requires that first the upper and then the lower ink form roller control levers be turned to the "on" position. Slight but important differences between the many offset presses in use today make it imperative that an operator commencing work on a new or unfamiliar machine obtain the instruction manual for that machine and study it with care.

Setting the Rollers

Of extreme importance in obtaining satisfactory results from the dampening system on an offset press is the amount and evenness of roller-to-roller and roller-to-plate pressure. Inadequate or uneven ductor-to-vibrator pressure can result in too little or erratic amounts of moisture transferred from the fountain roller to the oscillating vibrator roller. Excessive form dampening roller-to-plate pressure can cause flooding (too much moisture on the plate) and image wear. The pressure between the vibrator roller and the form roller also must be neither too great nor too small.

To test the pressure between the form dampening roller and the plate, place two 1 ″ wide strips of 20-lb. paper between the roller and the plate, one strip near each end of the roller. Turn the form roller control lever to the "on" position. Grasp both strips of paper and slowly pull them from between the roller and the plate. The operator should be able to withdraw the strips without tearing them by exerting a firm, uniform pull on each strip. An unequal drag on the strips indicates the roller is not set exactly parallel to the surface of the plate. If the strips strongly resist withdrawal, perhaps tear, the roller contacts the plate too heavily. If the strips of paper can be pulled out freely, with little or no drag, overall pressure between the roller and the plate should be increased.

Study the instruction manual carefully before attempting to adjust form dampening roller pressures. These adjustments are slightly different on different presses. On the ATF Chief 15, for instance, a simple lock nut adjustment directly over the roller's spindle controls roller pressure; adjustment is made at the end of the roller needing it or at both ends to increase or decrease overall pressure. This adjustment on the Addressograph-Multilith 1250 is somewhat more complicated. One adjustment raises or lowers the left end of the roller only; another adjustment, to the eccentric roller shaft, increases or decreases the roller's overall pressure.

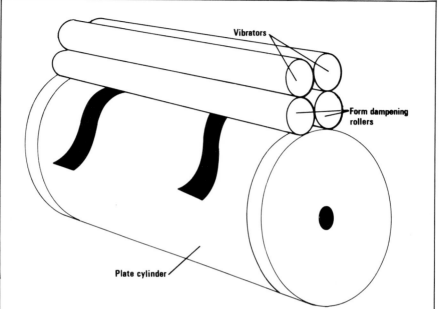

To test dampener roller-to-plate pressure settings, place strips of 20-lb. bond or plastic of similar weight between a roller and the plate, lower the roller into full contact with the plate, and pull on the strips' ends. Equal tension or resistance to pull should be felt on both strips of paper.

On A.B. Dick presses, a dampening roller does not contact the plate. Here, moisture control involves merely adjusting the ductor-to-vibrator roller pressure. Turn the machine over by hand until the ductor roller operating levers travel as far as they can toward the oscillator roller. Now adjust the eccentric screws until there is a 1/64" gap between the rollers, across their entire length. Check this gap whenever adjusting the pressure of the ink form rollers against the plate.

Adjustment of the pressure between the metal vibrator roller and the cloth-covered form dampening roller also may vary on those presses permitting such adjustment to be made. This may require turning an eccentric stud located in the press frame near one end of the vibrator roller, or raising or lowering the ends of the roller by means of a lock nut and screw and a roller spindle retainer. Insert two strips of paper between the vibrator roller and the form dampening roller, one strip at each end of the rollers, and test the resistance to pull. Adjust the vibrator roller pressure if necessary.

Usually the pull should be approximately equal on strips of paper placed between the form roller and the plate and on strips between the vibrator roller and the form dampening roller. For this reason it is advisable to make these two adjustments at the same time. Be sure to adjust the form dampening roller pressure first, however, as pressure from the vibrator roller can affect the paper-strip reading of the form roller pressure.

On those presses having two form dampening rollers, efficient moisture control may require slightly different pressure settings between the rollers. If the vibrator first in line to receive water from the fountain sets too heavily against its form dampening roller, this form roller may take up most of the moisture. The second form dampening roller would then suffer moisture starvation. Try setting the vibrator to the first form dampening roller with slightly less pressure than the vibrator to the second form roller.

The ductor roller plays a vital role in the dampening system and its settings cannot be overlooked. Try to obtain a setting of equal pressure between the ductor roller and the two rollers it contacts. The ductor roller usually needs to be adjusted in one direction only, to the fountain roller or the vibrator roller. Spring tension holds it in the desired pressure against the other roller. As with the other rollers in the system, be sure the ductor roller lies exactly parallel to the two rollers it contacts. Otherwise an uneven film of water transferred to the vibrator roller will lead to dampening problems of a serious nature.

With all the rollers properly adjusted, the dampening or fountain solution should form a thin film of moisture over all the non-image areas of the plate and effectively repel ink from these areas.

The Fountain Solution

Unless we use one of the relatively new alkaline based fountain solutions, the prepared mixture flowing through the dampening system to moisten the plate will contain certain acidic salts rather than alkali or alkaline salts.

Under normal circumstances and for most offset plates, the acid/alkaline rating or pH value of acid based fountain solutions (sometimes referred to as fountain etches) when fresh should test at between 4.0 and 5.5 on a scale reading from 1 to 14, with 7 being neutral. A solution having a reading below 4.0 may prove too acid, while a solution with a pH value much above 5.5 frequently is too far on the alkaline side of the acid/alkaline scale for optimum printing results. Excess acid in the fountain solution can cause several kinds of printing problems, not the least of which is failure of the printed ink film to dry properly. Excess alkalinity, on the other hand, can lead to serious plate scum as the protective film of gum arabic gives way to ink in the non-image areas of the plate.

This narrow tolerance — between 4.0 and 5.5 — explains why offset press technicians stress the importance of mixing up batches of fountain solution correctly and with extreme care and close attention to formula directions. Preparing a correctly balanced mixture is one of the most important defensive measures the operator can take to prevent printing difficulties caused by an incorrect pH value of the fountain solution.

The first step to take in mixing up a batch of fountain solution is to read the instructions on the fountain solution concentrate bottle. The concentrate recommended by one offset press manufacturer should be mixed at the rate of one ounce of concentrate to seven ounces of distilled water or 1/4 ounce of concentrate to 7 3/4 ounces of distilled water, depending on the type of ink to be used. Another brand of fountain solution concentrate works best when one ounce of the concentrate is mixed into 15 ounces of distilled water. Only by carefully reading and following the instructions can you hope to mix the concentrate, the water and/or other ingredients in correct proportions.

In preparing fountain solutions, be sure the mixing glasses or tumblers are absolutely clean and free of particles of dirt and dust or residues of previous mixings. Work in a well-lighted area, preferably over a sink where running water can wash away any spilled concentrate. Hold the measuring tumbler at eye level when pouring concentrate into it. This results in an accurate reading of the level of the liquid in the container. In addition, it avoids the possibility of your looking down into the tumbler while pouring chemicals into it, a none-too-safe practice. Take a reading of the level of water in the measuring tumbler in the same manner.

By taking accurate readings while mixing fountain solutions the operator can alter the solution's pH with some precision should unsatisfactory printing suggest such action. For instance, if the solution proves excessively acid, cutting back slightly on the amount of concentrate in the mix should increase the pH value to the desired level. Increasing the percentage of concentrate produces a more acid mixture.

As can be seen, the fountain solution pH initially depends on its composition; that is, the percentages of concentrate, water and other chemicals in the mix. When mixed as recommended by the supplier, the fountain solution usually will have the correct pH value. However, during the press run other factors—such as the pH of the paper being run—can alter the acidity of the solution. This

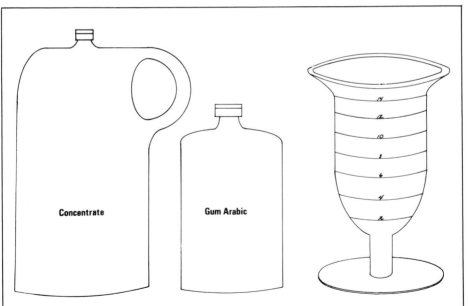

Concentrate

Gum Arabic

When preparing fresh fountain solution, carefully measure precise amounts of the different ingredients into clean, clearly marked measuring tumblers or mixing glasses.

means the operator must take periodic readings of the solution pH in order to maintain the correct acid/alkaline balance during a long press run.

The offset press operator plagued with excess fountain solution acidity may consider trying one of the "alkaline-based" fountain solutions, originally developed for short run lithographic reproduction of newspapers. On the market since about 1970, these solutions contain alkalies and alkaline salts rather than acids and acidic salts. Their pH value tends to run from 7 (neutral) to 10 or 11 on the pH scale. They are formulated for use without gum arabic, thus making it theoretically unnecessary to gum up the press plates during press stops and permitting somewhat faster press startups. In addition, their manufacturers—and a number of satisfied users— say the superior cleansing action of this type of fountain solution reduces paper piling and linting. It must be said that (at this writing) many companies strongly recommend the use on their press plates of solutions having a relatively acid pH value between 3.5 and 5.5. The various claims made for these new alkaline fountain solutions may nevertheless warrant a trial use by the operator. Be sure to purchase the solution or solution concentrate from a reliable supplier of lithographic materials.

In recent years offset press operators have shown considerable interest in the effect alcohol has on fountain solutions. Some of the larger offset presses now come equipped with "continuous" dampening systems that require alcohol in order to work. With smaller presses, it's largely a matter of individual preference, depending on whether the operator becomes convinced that adding alcohol to the fountain solution has a beneficial effect on printing quality or that it does not. Alcohol generally performs best in a mixture containing from 10% to 25% alcohol and 90% or 75% mixed fountain solution.

Dampening the Dampening System

Before filling the offset press fountain solution bottle or container, rinse all residues of old solution from it. At the same time, be sure that no solution from previous operations remains in the fountain tray, especially if the press has set idle overnight. Old fountain solution never works with the efficiency you expect of new solution; it only invites trouble to adulterate fresh solution with yesterday's mix.

With the fountain bottle filled, hold it upside down over the sink to be sure it does not leak unless the release valve is activated. Carefully place the bottle's spout in its receptacle on the press and observe the final level the water attains in the fountain. A faulty valve in the fountain solution bottle's spout will cause the fountain to overfill so that extra water splashes into the dampening system or onto the ink rollers.

Most dampening systems work best if slightly charged with moisture before actual printing commences. With the ink and dampener form rollers in the off position, let the press run for 20 or 30 revolutions to moisten the dampening rollers. Giving the fountain roller four or five complete turns by hand while the fountain roller and the ductor roller are in contact is a quick way to provide an initial dampening of the rollers. Don't overdo the matter, however. Just dampen the rollers, don't saturate them. Otherwise, an ink/water imbalance may cause problems from the very start of the press run.

Regulate the flow of fountain solution through the dampening system by setting the fountain roller control lever or knob at one of several fixed positions. These notched positions usually number from one to six. Best results are obtained with the control lever at the lowest setting that provides sufficient amounts of moisture for the dampening system. This usually turns out to be the second or third notch. Refer to the instruction manual for the press in use.

With the fountain solution accurately mixed in the recommended proportions of concentrate, water and other ingredients and with the dampening rollers properly adjusted and slightly charged with moisture, the press should be ready for the printing of the first few makeready copies of the job in progress.

Chapter 5
Press Makeready

Before the operator can begin any job of printing on the offset press, a process of press preparation called makeready must be undertaken. Unless the job in progress duplicates the preceeding job, makeready can involve several steps, from one end of the press to the other, some of them quite complicated.

The operator must recognize the importance of each one of the several steps of makeready. The operator can bypass none of them without jeopardizing the quality of presswork. Any part of off-set press makeready can prove to be the decisive factor in arriving at a successful completion of the job.

Securing the Plate to the Plate Cylinder

One of the steps often considered a part of press makeready, mounting the plate, has undergone previous examination. It will not hurt to review briefly some of the important points of this operation.

Before mounting the plate, carefully examine it for physical defects or photochemical or processing errors. Wipe both the plate and the plate cylinder surfaces clean and dry to be sure no moisture or lumps of dirt, dried ink or other hard foreign matter becomes trapped between the plate and the cylinder. With a micrometer, obtain a precise measurement of the plate's thickness. Where appropriate, add enough packing sheets to bring the image surface of the plate to cylinder bearer height or .001″ higher. Select new or undamaged sheets of underpacking and discard any patches of tissue paper left from previous makeready operations. Mount each new plate absolutely smooth and flat to the plate cylinder surface.

Seat the leading edge of the plate squarely into the lead clamping device and clamp it in place. Turn the press over by hand, keeping plate and packing sheets drawn tight and smooth to the cylinder surface. Secure the trailing edge of the plate with the rear clamping device. Re-angle the plate if necessary, moving the plate's leading edge laterally in one direction and the trailing edge in the other direction, to square the image with the plate cylinder and the sheet being printed.

Before submitting a fully secured plate to impression pressures, examine it for a bulge near its forward edge. Such a bulge, however slight, can develop into a plate-damaging crease or wrinkle during the first few revolutions of the press. A bulge near the forward edge of a new plate may appear if we neglect to return both the lead and rear clamping devices to a central or neutral position upon completion of the previous job. To eliminate the bulge, move the trailing edge of the plate to the right or to the left by adjusting the rear lateral adjustment device in the proper direction—to the left to correct a bulge on the right side of the plate, for instance.

Loading the Feeder Unit

Not all offset press operators begin makeready by mounting the plate. Some first load the feeder unit or lift with the paper cut for the job. Since handling cut paper requires clean hands, this partly determines when to perform this particular task. Quite often the operator finds it expedient to load the lift in a two-step operation, placing a portion of the cut stock in the lift before and the remainder after other makeready tasks have been completed. From 500 to 1,000 sheets are placed in the lift initially and just before actual printing commences the operator places the rest of the stock in the lift. This depends partly on the size of the job and the number of sheets the feeder unit will hold.

The lift on some small offset presses will handle no more than a stack of paper equal in height to a ream of 20-lb. bond. With these, the operator may safely fill the lift any time it runs empty or when he has clean hands. Little difficulty will be experienced in changing the position of the stack in the lift should minor adjustments prove necessary.

More commonly, offset press lifts accomodate 5,000 to 6,000 sheets of 20-lb. bond. This many sheets produces a stack of paper in excess of 15 inches high. If the operator fills the lift to capacity before completing other makeready operations, it may become necessary to move the whole pile in order to align the sheets with the plate image. It's nearly impossible to move a 15-inch stack of paper an inch to the left or the right without getting part of the stack off balance. As every seasoned press operator knows, nothing leads to paper feeding difficulties quicker than poorly stacked paper in the feeder unit.

Indeed, an offset press operator's expertise often can be judged simply by observing how he or she handles cut stock while placing it in the lift. An inexperienced operator, perhaps working under the pressure of swiftly passing minutes, may drop small batches of paper in the lift in a hurried and haphazard fashion. Then, during operation of the press, sheets may fail to separate properly or twist and tear in the feeder and run crookedly along the conveyor table to jam in the register guides. This may require several press stops to readjust the stack. The operator who handles paper with the care it deserves experiences far less trouble.

To set the feeder unit, take one of the sheets of cut stock and fold it in half lengthwise. Use the crease thus formed as a guide to position the sheet on the lift table. Lower the lift far enough to accept 500 to 1,000 sheets and place the folded sheet on the table. Position the sheet from 1/8″ to 3/8″ to the left or the right of center, away from the side guide in use on the conveyor table. Now bring the adjustable side and back guides of the feeder unit into alignment with the sheet's outside edges. Heavy card or bristol stock may require a 1/8″ clearance between the back guide and the trailing edge of the sheet. None of the guides should be set so as to bind the sheets in the stack.

The feeder unit will have forward guides against which the leading edge of the sheets will rest. On some machines, the forward guides are in the form of vertical channels that also act as forward side guides; set these to correspond with the paper's outside front edges. On presses having flat forward guides, position these guides halfway between the center crease in the sheet and the sheet's outside edges.

With side, rear and front guides positioned, place on the lift table several waste sheets the same size and weight as the stock being used. These waste sheets will find use during clean-up operations when you finish the job, and will serve as a base for the basic stack.

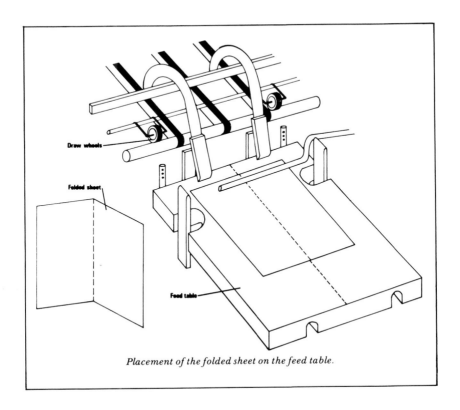

Draw wheels

Folded sheet

Feed table

Placement of the folded sheet on the feed table.

Before loading the feeder unit, examine the supply of cut paper planned for use to determine which way the edges of the sheets tend to curl. It's important to place all the stock for a given job in the lift either with the curl up or with the curl down. If feeder unit, conveyor table and register adjustments are made to accept sheets with the curl down, any sheets placed in the lift with the curl up will give trouble. Usually, but not invariably, paper feeds best through a press with the curl down.

Always handle paper with clean hands to avoid finger-printing any of the sheets. A liberal application of talcum powder on the hands and fingers just prior to handling paper often prevents smudges when the skin is moist.

Place the paper in the lift carefully, grasping no more than the number of sheets it is convenient to work with. Whether filling the lift to capacity or placing only two or three small batches in the lift, take time to riffle or fan each batch. This dislodges any paper fibers from the trimmed edges and separates sheets that sometimes get stuck together in the cutting operation. Use both hands to lower each batch directly onto the building stack, making sure all the sheets contact the front guides squarely. Avoid sliding batches of paper into the lift. This risks pushing one or more sheets from the top of the stack forward far enough to foul the leading edge of other sheets below. Make every effort to keep the stack straight and square.

Top the stack with a makeready "book." This consists of a dozen or so waste sheets, two or three clean sheets, another dozen waste sheets, more clean sheets, and so on, until you have four or five of these sets. All these sheets should have the same size, weight and grade as the paper planned for printing.

Setting the Paper Height Regulator

Turn the press over by hand to bring the paper height regulator to its lowest position. Now manually raise the lift to bring the top of the stack to within 1/8 " or 1/4 " of the thin metal sheet separators or "cat's whiskers" located at the front of the feeder unit. Adjust the paper height regulator to correspond to the top of the stack. During operation of the press, the top sheet in the stack should rise automatically to within 1/8 " to 1/4 " of the sheet separators — provided the paper height regulator is adjusted correctly for the stock being run. At this height the sheet separators limit the distance the air blowers can raise the top few sheets in the pile. Also, they prevent the lifting suckers from picking up more than one sheet at a time.

If the paper stack raises too high, the top sheets in the stack will foul the sheet separators and render them inoperative. If the stack fails to raise high enough, the lifting sucker feet cannot reach the top sheet and misfeeding will occur.

Refer to the instruction manual for the machine in use to locate the paper height regulator and its control mechanism. On some machines a thin metal blade or a small rod extends out over the stack in close proximity to the lifting suckers. The control knob should be located near a bend in the blade- or rod-type paper height regulator. On the A. B. Dick 350/360 models, four paper height regulators located behind the feeder unit's front plate also contain small holes through which blasts of air blow to separate the top sheets in the stack.

Some press manufacturers recommend setting the paper height regulator in the following manner: Lower the feeder unit one or two inches and turn on the power (but not the vacuum pump or air blowers). As the stack raises, adjust the paper height regulator control knob to stop the stack's upward movement when it reaches the recommended height below the sheet separators. This provides a good way to check the paper height regulator settings on most machines. Turn the power off when completed.

The sheet separators work best when evenly spaced along the leading edge of the sheet and close to the lifting sucker feet. If possible, position one directly in front of each lifting sucker foot. Adjust it to set level with the foot when the foot has reached its lowest position. Adjust these thin, flexible separators to extend from 1/8 " to 3/16 " out over the leading edge of the paper in the lift. Make sure they do not contact the lifting sucker feet.

These approximate adjustments will differ on different presses. Also, the actual requirements of a particular sheet size or weight of paper may force the operator to make minor paper height regulator and sheet separator settings after printing has commenced.

Lifting and Forwarding Suckers, Pullout Rollers and Air Blowers

When the paper stack has raised to the correct distance below the sheet separators, set the air blowers, the pickup and forwarding suckers and the pullout rollers.

Air forced through the blowers, usually positioned at the outside edges at the front of the stack, separates the top few sheets from the pile and floats the top-most sheet to enable the lifting suckers to make positive contact with it.

Set the blowers so the top second or third air hole in the tube is level with the top sheet in the stack, and the holes are directed diagonally across the stack. Switch on the vacuum pump and the blowers and observe how air introduced between the top sheets separates them from the stack. The air blast should feather no more than the top four to six sheets. The operator controls this action by raising or lowering the air blower tubes or by increasing or decreasing the amount of air blast directed at the sheets.

Leave the vacuum pump on and turn the machine over by hand until the lifting suckers make contact with the top sheet. The suckers should now be at their lowest point. Position the sucker feet equally along the leading edge of the sheet, behind the sheet separators. If the press has a single lifting sucker foot, center it on the sheet directly behind the multiple sheet detector and sheet separator.

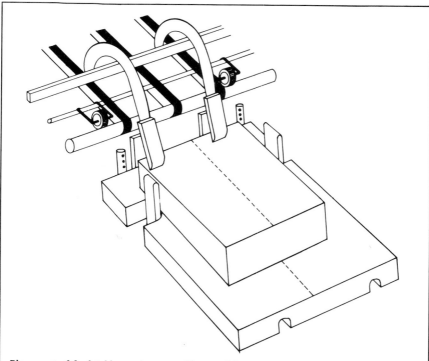

Placement of feed table components—blowers, lifting suckers, sheet separators, in relation to lift of the stock.

Continue to turn the machine over by hand until the lifting suckers pick up the air-feathered top sheet. Observe this action carefully. Proper timing of the feeder unit requires the pickup suction to begin at the bottom of the lifting suckers' downward stroke and continue to hold the sheet until the forwarding suckers or pullout rollers take over.

The forwarding suckers take the fully separated sheet from the lifting suckers and forward it into the pullout rollers (sometimes referred to as the draw wheels). The forwarding suckers should deliver the sheet squarely into the pullout rollers; occasionally, it will be necessary to adjust the angle of the forwarding suckers to accomodate the curl of the paper being printed. Not all offset presses have forwarding suckers. On many presses, the sheet transfers directly from the lifting suckers to the pullout rollers.

The upper and lower pullout rollers take the sheet from the lifting or forwarding suckers and deliver it to the conveyor tapes. Position the movable upper pullout rollers either inside or outside the lifting or forwarding sucker feet. The size and kind of paper being printed determines the location of the upper pullout rollers. In order for each sheet to be drawn forward squarely onto the conveyor belts, the tension of both pullout rollers should be the same. Unequal tension may twist the sheet and cause misregister. Test the tension by placing a strip of paper under each roller and withdrawing them. If necessary, adjust the tension so the withdrawal resistance of each pullout roller is equal. A light, even pressure, only enough to draw each sheet off the stack, usually proves most satisfactory.

Setting the Multiple-Sheet Detector

Most offset presses have a multiple sheet detector that, when properly set, prevents more than one sheet at a time from being forwarded into the register guides and printing cylinders. A double thickness of the paper being printed causes the detector to activate a metal plate or flap located in the conveyor table just ahead of the conveyor tapes. The plate deflects any doubles into a tray below the conveyor table. Whenever the operator changes from one weight of paper to another, a check of the multiple sheet detector setting may be in order.

Usually, the detector foot will be set directly over the lower pullout roller in a position near the center of the sheet being run. A micrometer adjusting knob moves the detector foot closer to or further from the lower pullout roller in increments of approximately .001 " per click or notch.

To set the multiple sheet detector, tear a strip of paper from a sheet of the stock being run and feed the strip between the detector foot and the lower pullout roller. With the drive motor on and the vacuum pump and air blast off, adjust the detector foot downward onto the strip of paper until it begins to activate the deflector plate. Now raise the detector foot one click at a time until the deflector plate no longer operates. Raise the detector foot an additional .001 " by turning the adjusting know one more click. To test the setting, fold the strip of paper in half and insert it between the detector foot and the lower pullout roller. This should immediately activate the deflector plate.

Conveyor Tapes, Hold-down Wheels, Balls or Straps and Register Guides

Switch the drive motor off. Position the movable conveyor tape guides so two or more of the conveyor tapes will run equally spaced under the sheet. These bracket-shaped tape guides through which the continuous tapes move are reached from above or below the conveyor table, depending on the machine. Be sure to position the outside tapes far enough in from the outside edges of the running sheet that these tapes do not foul the jogger or the side register guide. Turn the machine on briefly to allow the conveyor tapes to conform to the tape guide settings.

With the drive motor off, manually start a sheet down the conveyor table until it rests squarely against the forward guides or head stops.

Flat metal straps, steel ball races, glass marbles, metal tape rollers or wheels or a combination of these, are now positioned so as to hold the sheet flat and to assist the tapes in forwarding it into the register guides. Place the straps (or the ball races, on those machines having these paper control devices) over the outside conveyor tapes. Adjust the straps so they exert a light pressure against the sheet. Heavy paper tends to require more strap pressure than lightweight stock. Slightly more strap pressure against the sheet on the side nearest the side guide sometimes improves register of the sheet by preventing the formation of waves or wrinkles in it. Position the tape wheels over any two tapes an equal distance in from the sheet's outside edges, with the wheels just off the trailing edge of the sheet when the sheet has registered fully against the forward guides or head stops.

It is important to have some form of control on the sheet — metal straps, steel balls or marbles, tape wheels — before the sheet leaves the pullout rollers. Otherwise the sheet may start into the registering guides at an angle the tapes and control devices cannot overcome.

On some presses, the sheet is brought into register before entering the printing cylinders when a movable jogger on one side of the conveyor table pushes or jogs the sheet against a stationary guide on the other side. On other machines the side guide moves over toward the sheet far enough to grasp its edge and pull it into register against a stop. The sheet should move down the conveyor table from 1/8" to 1/4" away from the guide, as stated.

With the sheet resting squarely against the head stops, continue to turn the press over by hand until the jogger moves as far toward the sheet as it will go or until the side guide has pulled the sheet as far as it can. Using the positioning scale on the conveyor table, move the jogger or guide and the sheet toward the guide side of the table to bring the sheet into register with the image on the plate. Secure the jogger or side guide in place with the locking nut or screw. Most machines provide a means for making micrometer adjustments to the registering guide or jogger to permit "fine tuning" the sheet's register. Be sure the flat side of the jogger or guide exactly parallels the edge of the sheet when the sheet rests squarely against the head stops and the registering devices have been set.

As can be seen, if the sheet must be moved much further than 1/8" to 1/4" to bring it into register, the operator will have to reposition the stack in the feeder unit accordingly; hence the inadvisability of filling the lift to capacity until makeready is completed. Ideally, the off-centered sheet will be pushed or drawn into a central position on the conveyor belt by the registering jogger or guide.

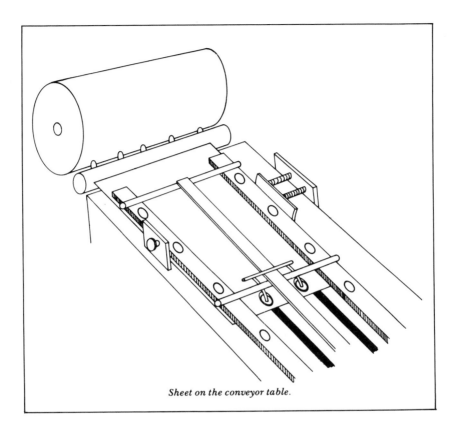

Sheet on the conveyor table.

With the conveyor belts, paper control devices and registering mechanism operating correctly, manually feed another sheet along the conveyor table toward the forward guides or head stops. As the sheet approaches to within 1/4″ to 3/8″ of the head stops these thin metal fingers at the end of the conveyor table should rise into position. At this point the feed rollers that draw the sheet directly into the printing cylinders should have moved apart. Continue turning the press over by hand until the sheet moves over into register position and the upper feed roller drops and pulls it forward into the cylinder grippers. Observe the sheet's progress into the printing cylinders. It should travel straight forward without twisting, buckling or wrinkling.

When the sheet falls into the delivery tray align the delivery joggers with the outside edges of the sheet. Use considerable care in adjusting the delivery joggers. Set them close enough to the sheet that they will jog the delivery stack into a neat, straight pile but not so tightly against the sheet that they will buckle the printed sheets and cause setoff or smearing of the image.

Bringing Up the Image

The final makeready step, bringing up the image, can be broken down into five parts.

1. *Ink up the inking rollers.* Switch on the drive motor and let the press run at slow speed while ink feeds forward from the ink fountain through the inking system. Do not lower the ink form rollers to the plate at this time.

2. *Wet the dampening system.* Engage the dampening ductor roller to charge the dampening system with a film of fountain solution. Do not lower the form dampening rollers to the plate at this time.

3. *Run a test sheet through the press.* Activate the vacuum pump and air blowers, and allow a single sheet to feed through the press in order to observe the action of the lifting suckers, the pullout rollers, the conveyor tapes and the register guides.

At this time determine whether the lifting sucker suction is correct for the stock being run. Suction requirements change for different weights of stock, more suction being necessary to lift heavy sheets from the paper stack than lightweight sheets. The lifting suckers should consistently pick up a single sheet of paper and deliver it squarely to the forwarding suckers or the pullout rollers. To obtain the correct suction:

    a. Turn the suction control valve back
to eliminate all suction to the lifting suckers.

    b. Let the machine bring the stack to
operating height.

    c. Gradually increase the suction, or lift,
of the lifting suckers until they pick up
a single sheet of the stock being printed.

    d. If necessary, increase the suction slightly
by giving the control knob an extra 1/4 turn.

4. *Pre-moisten the plate.* If the makeready steps for the job in progress promise to consume considerable time, the operator should plan to pre-moisten the plate on the press rather than on the work table prior to mounting it. Turn off the vacuum pump and stop the press. For best results, follow the plate manufacturer's recommendations for moistening the plate in use. Or, moisten the plate as suggested previously: use a sponge dampened with undiluted fountain solution for paper plates or with fountain solution diluted at the rate of 15 ounces of water to one ounce of mixed fountain solution for metal plates. Go over the entire surface of the plate. Moisten it but do not saturate it with fountain solution.

5. *Ink up the plate image.* Start the press again and make sure the dampening system is charged with water and the inking system carries a thin, even film of color. Lower the form dampening rollers to the plate. Let the press run for a few revolutions to be sure the plate receives adequate moisture, then lower the ink form rollers to the plate. Observe carefully how well the image accepts the ink to determine if the initial ink fountain settings need changing. Be sure the non-image areas of the plate remain free of any ink.

Some operators reverse the order recommended here by first lowering the ink form rollers and then the form dampening rollers to the plate. The individual operator must decide if this method works best on the initial roll-up of the plate.

First Printing

With the image fully inked, turn on the vacuum pump and activate the air blowers. Lower the plate cylinder into contact with the blanket cylinder. In contact or printing position the plate transfers an inked image, in reverse, onto the blanket. Let the press continue to run for three or four revolutions while a sharp image develops on the blanket surface.

Allow the first section of the makeready "book" to feed through the press, including the dozen waste sheets and one or two of the clean sheets. Turn off the paper feed. Raise the ink form rollers and the form dampening rollers, in that order, from the plate. Now turn on the paper feed again and run five or six more waste sheets through the press to run down the ink on the plate and blanket. Turn off the paper feed and take the plate cylinder off impression, or printing contact, with the blanket cylinder. Turn off the vacuum pump and switch off the drive motor. If sheet inspection time promises to last longer than 15 minutes, gum the plate by thoroughly wiping down its entire surface with the manufacturer-recommended plate gum, then polish the plate dry with a clean rag.

Examine one of the good sheets just printed to determine how much the ink or water must be changed, whether the image needs further straightening or should be brought into closer register. Pay particular attention to the density of the printed ink film. If the edges of the printed sheets have considerably more curl than the edges of the paper in the feeder unit, this is one indication excess water is being run to the dampening system. Adjust the flow of ink or fountain solution if necessary. Reposition the image, if it appears crooked on the sheet, following the steps given in Chapter 2.

Remember that ink and water adjustments take effect somewhat slowly. Offset press technicians recommend beginning with light ink and water settings, it being easier to increase than to decrease the flow of ink and fountain solution. Let the press idle for several revolutions to allow adequate time for any ink or water adjustments made to become apparent on the plate.

With the necessary adjustments made, wash the gum off the plate and repeat Step 5 given under "Bringing up the Image." Lower the plate cylinder into contact with the blanket cylinder. Let the image on the blanket become sharp and clear. Now run another section of the makeready "book" through the press and examine the good sheets for printing errors. Do this as often as necessary to obtain an acceptable imprint on the sheets.

When completely satisfied with the results of the makeready efforts, finish placing the remainder of the paper cut for the job in the lift, set the counter at 0 and commence the run. It's usually best to begin a run at lower press speeds and gradually increase the speed as printing progresses. Remember to change press speeds exactly in the way the press manufacturer recommends. On some presses it is necessary to stop the press, adjust the speed control, then start the press again. On other machines, change the printing speed only with the press in operation to avoid placing unnecessary strain on the speed control mechanism.

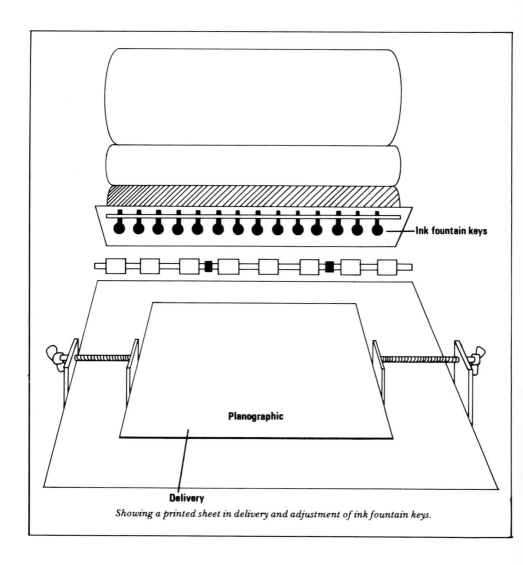

Ink fountain keys

Planographic

Delivery

Showing a printed sheet in delivery and adjustment of ink fountain keys.

End of Operation

At the end of the press run, follow the procedure outlined above to run down the ink on the plate and the blanket, using the waste sheets first placed in the lift for this purpose. Wash the blanket with the recommended blanket wash, using only enough solvent to remove the image from the blanket's surface.

The plate can be left overnight by gumming it and wiping it dry on the press as described above.

If the plate is to be put in storage, remove it from the press and clean excess ink from the image with a mild solvent, preferably the cleaning agent recommended by the manufacturer. Rinse the plate under running water to wash away all traces of the solvent. Now place the plate on a dry, smooth surface and gum its entire surface with a liberal amount of plate gum. Use a clean, disposable wipe to buff the gum smooth and dry. Be sure the back side of the plate is dry, then store the plate in a dry, protected area. Store plates either face-to-face or back-to-back with sheets of tissue between them.

Follow the above procedure for metal plates. Handle paper plates as recommended by the manufacturer for the specific type of plate in use.

The operator should consider these makeready and operating procedures as a basic guide. Study the instruction manual for a particularly intricate phase of makeready. These instructions differ in detail from press to press. But if press makeready follows a logical, step-by-step sequence similar to the suggestions given here, the offset press operator will move through the necessary steps in the minimum amount of time and will more consistently produce presswork of a professional quality.

Chapter 6
The Printing Cylinders

Most offset presses have three printing cylinders—the plate, the blanket and the impression cylinders. Some machines, such as the Davidson Dualith, have two printing cylinders, one approximately twice the diameter of the other. The larger cylinder on a two-cylinder press doubles as both plate and impression cylinder.

With the plate and blanket cylinders packed to specifications, the operational efficiency of the printing cylinders depends upon two factors—cylinder-to-cylinder pressure, and cylinder maintenance and repair. In the absence of correct pressure settings between the plate and blanket cylinders and between the blanket and impression cylinders, the operator cannot hope to consistently produce high quality work on an offset press.

Plate-to-Blanket Pressure

Before altering the pressure between the plate and blanket cylinders, check the present pressure setting to be sure a change is desirable or necessary.

Technicians recommend checking plate-to-blanket pressure setting only after having checked the ink form roller pressure settings. Printing problems such as a fading image can result from excessively light ink roller settings as well as from insufficient cylinder pressure. With the form dampening rollers in the "off" position and each fully inked form roller should leave on the plate surface a band from 1/8″ wide on small presses to 3/16″ wide on larger presses. The ink bands should be uniformly wide from one end to the other across the plate.

An ink band produced on the blanket by an inked plate similarly provides the means for checking the plate-to-blanket pressure. With the form dampening rollers in the "off" position and the ink form rollers in the "on" position, start the press and ink up the entire plate. Ink should cover both the image and non-image areas of the plate in a thin, even film.

Stop the press with the inked plate and the blanket opposite one another. Gently lower the plate into full printing contact with the blanket. Now raise the plate cylinder and turn the press over by hand until the band imprinted on the blanket comes into view.

The band should appear uniformly wide across the blanket. The proper width of the band depends partly on the size of the press in use and partly on the number of packing sheets placed under the blanket and the plate. Normally the band should be from 1/8 " wide on small presses to 3/16 " wide on larger presses. Refer to the instruction manual for the press in use for the correct band width to aim for.

In general, a band not much wider than 1/8 ", indicating light cylinder-to-cylinder pressure, is preferred to a wider band for optimum printing results.

To assure accuracy in checking pressure settings, repeat the above procedure a number of times, on different sections of the blanket. The average width of the several bands should provide a reasonably accurate assessment of plate-to-blanket pressure. Remember that insufficient or excessive amounts of underpacking can radically affect the ink band's width; it may pay to double-check the number of packing sheets under the plate and the blanket. Also an older blanket that has absorbed considerable moisture may swell enough to affect the apparent pressure setting or some areas of an older blanket may have become compressed through rough usage. Press manufacturers usually recommend making pressure setting checks with a new blanket installed on the machine.

On most presses plate-to-blanket pressure settings are changed by adjusting pressure control devices located on the operator's side of the machine. A locking nut or screw holds the adjusting knob, lever or screw in place. Loosen the locking screw and turn the adjusting screw fractionally clockwise or counterclockwise to change the pressure setting. The location of the adjustment device varies from machine to machine and the direction of movement, or turn, to increase or decrease plate-to-blanket pressure settings also varies. The adjustment device may raise or lower the plate cylinder or it may raise or lower the blanket cylinder. For these reasons it is vital that the operator study the instruction manual for the machine in operation before attempting to change this important setting.

On some machines such as the A. B. Dick 360, this adjustment is somewhat complicated and unless the operator has had considerable experience with these presses it is recommended that the manufacturer's service representative perform this operation, at least the first time it becomes necessary.

In addition to correct cylinder-to-cylinder pressures, both the plate and blanket cylinder surfaces must set exactly parallel to each other. The ink band imprinted on the blanket enables the operator to determine whether or not a serious angular displacement exists between the cylinders. If the band measures wider at one end than the other, the two cylinders obviously are not setting parallel to one another. Even the slightest difference in ink-band width can indicate cylinders far enough out of alignment to adversely affect the quality of the reproduction.

An uneven band could indicate uneven underpacking, of course, so the operator should briefly check the lay of the packing sheets. Another cause of unparallel cylinder settings often is nothing more than encrusted dirt or ink on the cylinder bearers or dirt imbedded in the cylinder gear teeth. A thorough cleaning of these areas should coincide with the pressure setting check.

An alternate method used by many offset press technicians for checking parallel and pressure settings between the plate and blanket cylinders involves examining the cylinder bearers. Since these two cylinders are designed to rotate with bearer-to-bearer contact, the bearer surfaces should appear relatively shiny, with few or no signs of corrosion or rust. Bearers shiny only in the area of the cylinder gaps may indicate that excessive underpacking is preventing complete bearer-to-bearer contact when the blanket and plate meet. To further check surface contact between the bearers, place several small dabs of ink on both bearers of one of the cylinders and turn the press over by hand with the cylinders on impression. Ink should transfer evenly from one cylinder to the other if the bearers ride in contact during printing as they should.

The plate and blanket cylinders on most small offset presses are factory-set parallel to each other. Any necessary changes should be made by a qualified factory serviceman.

The Davidson Dualith and some other presses permit small changes in plate-to-blanket cylinder pressure at one end of the cylinder only. This permits the operator to bring the cylinders parallel to each other. One end of the blanket (or plate, depending on the press) cylinder is raised or lowered to increase or decrease the width of the ink band at that end. When the band appears absolutely even from one side of the blanket to the other, the two surfaces will be exactly parallel. Once the cylinders have been aligned, the operator should again check the overall plate-to-blanket cylinder pressure, using the ink-band method described above.

Blanket-to-Impression Cylinder Pressure

Unlike the plate and blanket cylinders, the impression cylinder does not have bearers at the ends to contact the blanket cylinder bearers. The precisely ground surface of the impression cylinder contacts the blanket by body or surface pressure entirely; pressure settings do not depend on bearer-to-bearer contact.

To obtain sharp, clear reproductions, the pressure between the blanket and impression cylinders may have to be changed frequently. The impression cylinder must squeeze each sheet against the blanket surface with enough pressure to transfer the inked image from the blanket onto the paper or other printing surface. The weight, or thickness, of the sheet being run determines the amount of squeeze necessary to assure full transfer of the image. Thin, lightweight sheets require more pressure than do heavier sheets.

Most offset presses come from the factory with the impression cylinder pressure set for 20-lb. stock. This pressure setting may accommodate paper somewhat heavier or lighter than 20-lb. without lowering the quality of the print. Manufacturers of the A.B. Dick 350/360 series claim that for most stocks the impression cylinder pressure on these machines adjusts automatically to correspond to the requirements of the stock being printed. However, a rough-textured stock may require more pressure than normal for the particular weight or thickness of that stock in order to insure quality control of halftones and solids in the print. The surface texture of any paper may in fact significantly affect impression pressure requirements.

To adjust the impression cylinder pressure setting, when going from a lightweight stock to heavier paper, first back off the pressure until the printed image appears light, indicating insufficient print-ing pressure. Then gradually increase the pressure until the image prints sharp and clear with no broken characters or lines. This method prevents your accidentally providing excessive pressure be-tween the blanket and impression cylinders.

When operating the press with excessive impression pressure or running a heavy paper without reducing the pressure, the con-tinued heavy pressure subjects the blanket and the plate to undue wear. Poor reproduction quality also follows excessive blanket-to-impression cylinder pressure, the heavier pressure tending to broaden and distort fine lines and halftone dots.

When a change is made to paper less than 20-lb. in weight, the transferred image may appear light or indistinct and have broken lines or characters in the copy. This usually indicates insufficient impression cylinder pressure. Before changing the pressure setting, however, check the ink form roller pressure setting, the distribution of ink across the image areas of the plate and the plate-to-blanket pressure setting. These also have their individual and accumulative effect on the quality of the print.

As with plate-to-blanket cylinder pressure, blanket-to-impression cylinder pressure control devices are located at the side of the press opposite one of the cylinders. Read the operator's manual for the machine in use before performing this operation. Loosen the indicated locking screw and turn the adjusting screw in the proper direction to increase or decrease the pressure.

On the A.B. Dick 350/360 series machines the pressure is changed by removing the hand wheel, inserting an Allen wrench in the control dial opening and simply dialing the desired pressure with the aid of the numbered dial. On some machines such as the Davidson presses, impression cylinder pressures are controlled in a different manner. A metal drawsheet covers the impression segment of the plate/impression cylinder. Packing sheets placed beneath the drawsheet control the impression pressure. Insert packing sheets ac-cording to specifications in the instruction manual.

Some technicians recommend adjusting the impression cylinder pressure in a different manner from that described above. First cut two strips of paper approximately two inches wide and eight inches long from the stock to be printed. With the impression on, inch the press around until the impression cylinder grippers and the chain delivery grippers meet. Back off the impression cylinder pressure and insert the two strips of paper between the impression cylinder and the blanket, one strip near each side of the blanket. Now gradually increase the impression cylinder pressure until a slight, even drag on each strip of paper is felt. Pressure between the two cylinders now should be correct for the stock being run to within a few thousandths of an inch. Further minor adjustments to the impression cylinder pressure can be made after examining the first printed makeready sheets.

Detecting Cylinder Surface Damage

The surface areas of the printing cylinders on a new press have been factory-ground for precision printing. Any uneven, excessively blotchy or broken printing usually indicates improper pressure settings between the cylinders, faulty ink distribution, a defective blanket or inadequate or excessive underpacking—or a combination of two or more of these factors.

On some older presses or on a press that has sustained unusual wear or has been damaged, however, uneven printing may indicate the presence of dents or low spots in the surface of one or more of the cylinders. To eliminate the other possible sources of weak spots in the image, install a new blanket, a new plate, fresh underpacking and check the three printing cylinders and the ink form rollers for proper pressure settings. If uneven or weak areas of identical size and configuration continue to fall in the same area on the printed sheets, we may suspect a damaged cylinder as the cause.

Before attempting to assess the feasibility of repairing it, first determine which of the three cylinders has sustained the damage. Unless the dent or low spot can be located by visual or tactile inspection, proceed to discover the defective cylinder through a systematic process of elimination.

First remove the plate and blanket and thoroughly clean the three cylinder surfaces. Use a cleaning solvent strong enough to remove all the gum, dirt or dried ink from each cylinder. At the same time clean the plate and blanket cylinder bearer surfaces and scrub out any accumulated dirt, gum or dried ink from the cylinder gear teeth. Any hard foreign substance adhering to a cylinder surface can prevent complete contact between it and the corresponding cylinder surface. And lumps of dried ink or hard-packed dirt on the bearers or between any of the gear teeth can easily prevent full contact between the plate and blanket cylinders.

Technicians recommend examining the cylinders for damage in the following order: plate cylinder, blanket cylinder, impression cylinder.

Plate Cylinder Check: With the plate and any packing sheets removed and the cylinder surface perfectly clean, ink up the rollers with a medium film of black ink. Be sure the ink distributes evenly across the inking rollers. Run the press at slow speed and gently lower the best ink form roller until it contacts the plate cylinder. Let the press turn over several times to allow the metal surface of the cylinder to become fully inked. Lift the form roller and switch off the press.

Now slowly turn the press over by hand and examine the entire film of ink deposited on the plate cylinder. Look for ruptures, broken areas or light spots. These lightly inked or uninked areas pinpoint any dents or low spots in the cylinder surface. If the position of these lightly inked areas coincide with similar light areas on the printed sheets, you can feel reasonably certain a damaged plate cylinder is the cause of uneven printing and that the defects have been located.

If the film of ink deposited on the plate cylinder surface reveals no noticeably light or uninked areas, proceed to examine the other cylinders for damage.

Blanket Cylinder Check: Thoroughly clean the blanket cylinder, including surface, bearers and gear teeth, removing all traces of hardened gum, dirt and dried ink. Install a new blanket, or one known to be undamaged in any way; a defective blanket will produce light areas in the printed image much in the same way a damaged blanket cylinder will.

Pack the blanket to .002" above cylinder bearer height to create a normal printing squeeze between the plate and blanket. Wash the ink from the plate cylinder and install a blank press plate. Place enough packing material under the plate to bring it to .001" above cylinder bearer height.

With the dampening rollers in the "off" position, lower the ink form rollers to the plate and ink up its entire surface area. Be sure the plate bears a thin, even film of ink with no light areas visible; these would indicate a defective or improperly installed plate or a damaged plate cylinder. Place the press on "print" or "impression" and pull an impression on the blanket.

Switch off the press and turn the machine over by hand to examine the film of ink deposited on the blanket. Look for light or broken areas caused by insufficient pressure between plate and blanket. These lightly inked areas indicate either a defective blanket or a damaged blanket cylinder surface.

Before going further, run a blank sheet of paper through the press, one large enough to contain all the lightly inked areas showing on the blanket. A high-quality print is not necessary; just a print good enough to show the location and general shape of the light areas. Set this sheet aside for later reference. Some operators prefer to lay a sheet of tracing paper on the inked blanket and trace the outlines of the light areas on the thin paper.

The next step determines whether the low spots are in the blanket or in the cylinder surface. Wash the blanket and wipe it dry. Remove the blanket from the cylinder, turn it end-for-end and replace it, along with enough underpacking to bring it to .002 " above bearer height as before. Ink up the plate again and pull another impression on the blanket. Switch off the press and turn the machine over by hand to examine the lightly inked areas on the blanket, comparing their location and general size and shape with the light areas on the previously imprinted sheet or the outlines on the tracing paper.

If these light areas have followed the turning of the blanket on the cylinder, the blanket itself is demonstrably defective and should be repaired or replaced. If the light areas on the blanket or on a second imprinted sheet correspond in position with those on the first sheet, that is if they have remained stationary on the turned blanket in relation to the cylinder, the cylinder surface undoubtedly has dents or low spots.

Impression Cylinder Check: If the preceding checks fail to locate the cause of uneven printing, examine the impression cylinder surface for dents or low spots.

Clean the impression cylinder and the blanket surface and set the impression cylinder for maximum pressure. It may be wise to utilize the paper-strip method described under "Blanket-to-

Impression Cylinder Pressure" to set the pressure, using strips of lightweight tissue paper initially, then increasing the pressure slightly to insure maximum blanket-to-impression cylinder pressure.

Ink up the plate and pull another impression on the blanket. At least briefly, again examine the ink film deposited on the plate and blanket for any serious ruptures or lightly inked areas. It may be necessary to increase the ink flow or pull several impressions on the blanket to obtain a strong film of ink.

With the blanket fully and evenly inked, switch off the press, place the machine on "print" and turn it over by hand to transfer a solid film of ink from the blanket to the impression cylinder. If press controls permit gradually bringing the blanket and impression cylinders into printing contact. This operation can be performed with the power on instead of by hand.

Stop the press, then turn it over by hand to examine the ink film deposited on the impression cylinder. Any areas devoid of ink pinpoint low spots in the cylinder's surface.

Cylinder Surface Repair

Once any low spots have been located in a cylinder's metal surface, usually further assessment of the situation can be made by brushing the damaged surface with your fingertips. Whether to replace or repair the cylinder depends on the seriousness of the damage. An extensively dented or badly warped cylinder probably should be replaced. Efforts to repair badly damaged cylinders often prove wasteful of time and seldom renew the cylinder surface sufficiently to justify the expense.

Usually, damage sustained by a cylinder admits to repair with one of the commercial metal repair kits. Dents and depressions small in area can be built up to printing height with metal spraying and careful regrinding and polishing. Used correctly, a metal filler produces a permanent repair.

Some operators have used shellac and tissue paper with considerable success in emergency situations. Pieces of tissue paper are glued into place with shellac, each tissue larger than the one beneath it. Gradually the dent is built up to correspond with the surrounding surface area of the cylinder. Depending on the extent and location of the dent or low spot and how heavily the machine is used in normal operation, a shellac/tissue paper patch may hold in place long enough before needing a replacement to make this approach worth the effort. Be sure to sand the paper-and-shellac patch smooth once the shellac has dried to avoid creating a bulge in place of an indentation.

The operator who maintains precision surfaced or repaired cylinders, proper cylinder pressure settings and correct underpacking, insures continued production of commercial quality printing on the offset press.

Chapter 7
The Offset Blanket

The modern offset blanket, greatly improved over its predecessors, remains an essential part of the offset printing process as first conceived and developed by Ira Rubel in the early years of this century. The flexible, wrap-around, rubber-surfaced blanket permits an indirect transfer of the inked image from plate to blanket and then to the moving sheet being forwarded through the press. This indirect or offset printing physically separates the thin metal or paper plate from the wearing effect of continuous contact with the abrasive surface of the material being printed. At the same time, the rubber offset blanket provides a higher fidelity of image transfer than did older methods of lithographic printing.

In short, without the smooth surface of the rubber offset blanket, printing by lithographic processes probably never would have proved practical, much less have become the increasingly important craft that finds such widespread use today.

A basic understanding of its physical properties and of present day methods of manufacture enables the offset press operator to realize more fully the importance of selection, of preparation and of care of the offset blanket.

Manufacturing the Blanket
The offset blanket consists of two quite dissimilar segments, a fabric backing and a rubber surface, both bonded together into a single, flat, fairly thick flexible mat.

The fabric segment of the offset blanket has two or more layers or plies of fabric manufactured to strict specifications on special textile looms. The textile mills that produce these fabric backing plies generally use the finest long staple cotton available. Unusual printing requirements that demand greater blanket strengths require the use of strong synthetic yarns in the weaving process. Once woven, the fabric undergoes a process of machine stretching to eliminate most of the crimp or wave of the warp threads. This careful stretching in the direction of the warp mechanically "sets" the fabric and prevents gradual elongation of the blanket during its use on the press. A good offset blanket should have a stretch factor of less than two percent.

Depending primarily upon the final blanket thickness desired, the fabric backing may have two, three, four, or more layers of fabric. A specially prepared rubber cement laminates the layers, or plies, of fabric together to form what manufacturers call the "fabric carcass." The blanket manufacturer must exercise extreme care in laminating the several fabric layers together in order to produce a fabric carcass of an exact, pre-determined ply depth.

Finally, the readied fabric carcass receives the rubber surface segment of the blanket.

Most offset blankets in use today have synthetic rubber surfaces that strongly resist the deteriorating effects of the various solvents and chemical compounds that commonly come in contact with them. Natural rubber, found on all offset blankets prior to World War II, has a much lower tolerance to the various driers, ink vehicles and blanket washes used in offset printing and so finds limited application in the industry today.

The synthetic rubber compound, scientifically formulated and mixed to the consistency of a thick paste, is machine spread onto the fabric carcass in many thin layers. The rubber spreading or coating machine applies between 80 and 100 separate layers of the rubber paste. This insures an overall uniform density and precise thickness of the blanket's rubber surface.

This thickness may vary .001 " more or less than the standard .020 " depth set for the rubber surface of offset blankets. The manufacturer must hold closely to this fairly rigid tolerance. A variation of much more than .001 " above or below .020 " may result in a heavy, unstable surface or a surface thin enough to permit the weave design of the fabric backing to show up in the printed image.

An offset blanket may have a thickness, or gauge, of .050 ", .065 " or .075 " when finished, depending upon the undercut of the blanket cylinder of the press for which it has been designed. The manufactured gauge of the finished blanket should vary less than .002 " from the designated blanket thickness. Nothing better illustrates the care and precision with which blanket manufacturers work than the fact that the average offset blanket varies in thickness no more than between .0015″ and .001″ from the standards set by the industry.

The laminated and fully coated blanket finally undergoes a curing or vulcanizing process. This treatment increases the elasticity and strength of the blanket's rubber surface and has a great deal to do with the blanket's eventual serviceability. Rigid control of the vulcanizing process is necessary to prevent excessive hardness of the rubber.

Because of the different rubber compounds used in blanket manufacturing as well as the varying degrees of rubber hardness obtainable in the vulcanizing process, the offset press operator has a relatively wide range of blankets from which to choose. A manufacturer can offer a hard, medium or soft blanket surface composed of synthetic rubbers that will resist to a remarkable degree the effects of specific inks and solvents used in a particular plant.

Hard blankets promote cleaner, sharper printing on smooth or coated stock while decreasing the incidence of paper packing. Medium or soft blankets work best with coarse or rough surfaced papers; the softer rubber more positively transfers the image down into the valleys of the paper surface without excessive blanket-to-impression cylinder pressure. Though a medium-hard, all-purpose blanket consistently will produce high quality work under a wide variety of circumstances, the offset press operator using it should bear in mind the availability of hard or soft blankets designed for special printing purposes.

In the critical area of resistance to chemicals and solvents, for instance, if possible choose a blanket designed to withstand the effects of the inks or solvents that most likely will contact its surface. Be sure the supplier of offset blankets knows the type of inks used in the plant—linseed oil inks, hydrocarbon inks, etc. Some manufacturers offer blankets designed to overcome special printing difficulties such as the incidence of a condition similar to gear streaks, where an overpacked blanket tends to slip or skid when in contact with the plate and cause streak-like defects in the print.

To summarize, look for the following desirable characteristics in an offset blanket:

1. Little or no stretch after initial break-in.

2. Absence of high or low spots in the new blanket. The thickness or gauge should be the same over the entire area of the blanket and vary no more than plus or minus .001 ".

3. Resiliency sufficient to return the blanket to its normal thickness immediately following each impression.

4. Strength adequate to resist the day-to-day pressures, abuses, smashes and stretching to which normal printing processes subject a blanket.

5. Resistance to the effects of the chemicals and ingredients that come into contact with it.

6. Satisfactory ink receptivity and total image transfer.

7. Long mileage.

Blanket Care

The physical characteristics most desirable for high quality offset presswork, though inherently present in the majority of offset blankets made today, will prove of little value if we fail to give blankets the care and handling they deserve. Proper care of an offset blanket commences on the day it arrives at the printing plant.

Preparing the Blanket: When a new blanket arrives from the manufacturer, remove it from its fiberboard shipping tube and lay it on a flat surface in a cool, dark area. Avoid placing heavy objects on the blanket in an attempt to hold it flat. Prolonged compressing or pinching of a blanket often results in an irreparable surface distortion. Two or more blankets can be stored one on top of the other *provided* they are not stored with the fabric backing of one in direct contact with the rubber surface of the other. Store them back-to-back or face-to-face. This avoids any chance of patterning the rubber surface of one blanket with the weave of the fabric backing of the other.

If possible, leave the blanket or blankets thus stored for at least a week before mounting. Left unweighted and protected from the effects of sunlight and heat, a blanket will remain in good condition for a year or longer. Many technicians advise hanging a blanket from pegs or clips rather than leaving it lay flat after the initial flattening or "roll" relaxation. If necessary, of course, you can store blankets in old shipping tubes for long periods, a single blanket to a tube with the tube stood on end.

Mounting the Blanket: Proper mounting or fitting of an offset blanket to the blanket cylinder also comprises an important part of blanket care.

The blankets designed for a great many small sheetfed presses come from the manufacturer cut to size and factory punched. The operator fits or mounts a pre-cut, ready-punched blanket directly to the blanket cylinder, being careful to follow the directions in the instruction manual for the press in use.

Blankets for larger offset presses may arrive from the factory pre-cut to size but without holes drilled in the ends to accommodate the mounting bars. The operator must drill or punch the necessary number of holes.

Whether such a blanket appears rectangular or square, be sure to determine its top (leading) and bottom (trailing) edges before working on it. This is done by ascertaining the grain direction of the fabric backing. The grain coincides with the direction of the warp threads in the fabric. The blanket manufacturer usually stamps the grain direction on the back of the blanket or uses warp threads of a contrasting color.

A correctly mounted blanket will have these threads running around the cylinder, in the direction of cylinder movement. With the pre-stretched grain or warp direction running around the cylinder, a blanket will withstand mounting and printing tensions with minimal size distortion.

Having determined the blanket's top and bottom edges, lay it fabric side up on a clean, flat surface. Now draw a perfectly straight vertical line in the center of the blanket, from the top edge to the bottom edge. This line should run precisely parallel to or overlay one of the warp threads. With the aid of a steel square, draw two horizontal lines at right angles to this center line, one horizontal line ½ " to 1 " back from the top edge of the blanket and the second line ½ " to 1 " from the bottom edge. The actual distance from the blanket's edges to place these lines will vary according to the cut length of the blanket and the distance desired between the mounting bars.

Place the outer edge of a mounting bar at one of the horizontal lines. This will indicate where holes should be marked and drilled (or punched) to correctly secure the mounting bars to the blanket.

By working from accurately drawn positioning lines, drilling holes across the blanket in a line that corresponds to a possibly unparallel blanket edge is avoided. The horizontal lines will lie parallel to each other and so will the drilled holes and the secured mounting bars. In addition, the mounting bars will lie at right angles to the warp threads in the blanket's backing.

It should be noted that many technicians recommend punching or drilling the holes in a slight arc or bow across the blanket. Each line of holes should bow away from the center of the blanket and toward the nearest edge, with the center holes drilled marginally closer to the blanket's top and bottom edges than the four corner holes and with the corner holes drilled equally from the horizontal positioning lines. This arrangement of drilled holes imparts somewhat more tension at the blanket's sides. For blankets up to 36" wide, aim for an arc of approximately 1/8", and an arc of 1/4" for blankets up to 72" wide.

With either a straight or bowed line of holes, it is important that the mounting bars lie exactly parallel to each other to avoid drawing one side of the blanket tighter than the other during mounting operations.

Before mounting the blanket to the blanket cylinder, determine how much underpacking the blanket requires to bring it to cylinder bearer height. Use the hand micrometer with care to discover the blanket's true thickness. Inaccurate use of a micrometer can result in a thickness reading as much as .003" less than the blanket's actual thickness. This may lead you to place excessive amounts of packing under the blanket which may cause overpressure between the plate and the blanket. The Graphic Arts Technical Foundation offers a blanket thickness gauge that many offset press operators prefer over the hand micrometer.

Most technicians recommend packing the blanket cylinder to .002" above cylinder bearer height. This, plus a corresponding .001" overpacking of the plate cylinder results in a .003" impression squeeze between blanket and plate.

With the blanket gauged for thickness and the packing sheets readied, secure the blanket to the leading edge of the blanket cylinder as outlined in the instruction manual. Depending on the type and size of press, the blanket securing device will be in the form of a clamping bar, pins corresponding to pre-drilled holes in

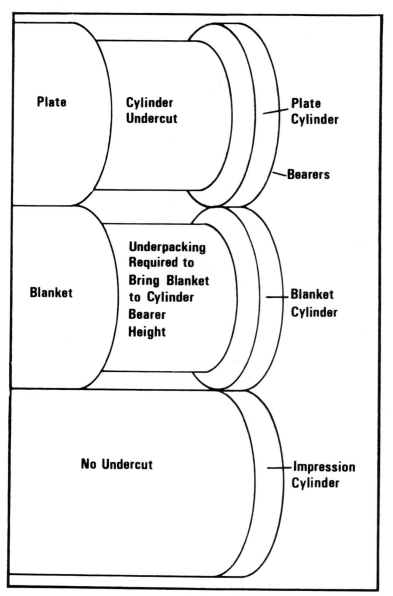

*Underpacking is required to bring the blanket to cylinder bearer height. Size of under-
cut is exaggerated in illustration to demonstrate the situation.*

factory-finished blankets, a blanket tightening reel, or other clamping device. Insert the packing sheets well up under the secured leading edge of the blanket. Turn the press over by hand or inch it forward with the jogging button while keeping the blanket and packing sheets pressed tight and even against the blanket cylinder surface. It may help to have the cylinders on impression until the blanket's trailing edge can be secured. When the rear edge of the cylinder moves into position, secure the trailing edge of the blanket to the rear clamping device.

The next step, tightening the blanket, that is stretching it taut between the clamping devices, determines to a large extent how long the blanket will provide top performance transfer of the image. By all means avoid overtightening a blanket during initial installation procedures. This tends to compress the individual fibers in the fabric backing and may create artificial but permanent low spots in the blanket. Overtightening a blanket may even forcibly separate some of the warp threads and lead to an early breakdown of the fabric backing.

Draw the blanket up snug, realizing that some stretch will remain. Technicians recommend the use of a torque wrench, which permits tightening a blanket to an initial, pre-determined degree of tension. After a careful washup of the blanket, run the press slowly, on impression, for approximately 50 revolutions. Stop the press and draw the blanket tighter by an additional notch. Repeat this once or twice if necessary and again after 1,000 to 1,500 impressions of the first job printed with the new blanket.

Cleaning the Blanket: Few operations prove more important to the well-being and length of utility of an offset blanket than the methods used to clean it.

A new blanket will have on its surface a fine powder or sulphur "bloom," a residue of the manufacturing process that the operator should remove before putting the blanket into service. Use the wash recommended by the blanket manufacturer or a petroleum distillate having a boiling point between 190° F and 265° F. Any distillate used should contain no oily residue.

Avoid cleaning solvents such as kerosene, benzol, ketone, toluene, xylene and mineral spirits on offset blankets. Avoid using gasoline that contains lead; white gas, though used in many printing plants, is recommended by few if any blanket manufacturers. Never use carbon tetrachloride or carbone disulphide, for the sake of your own health as well as that of the blanket. If turpentine or pine oil or similar oxidizing fluids are used on a blanket, an undesirable tackiness or glaze can be expected to develop on the rubber surface. The operator may have no recourse but to replace the blanket after using such a surface treatment over a period of time.

To repeat: Use the blanket wash recommended by the blanket manufacturer to prevent early deterioration of the blanket surface. Wash the blanket as infrequently as possible. Excessive washups increase the chance of moisture running under the edges of the blanket and working its way into the fabric backing. This causes an immediate swelling of the blanket and may eventually impair the bond between the fabric backing and the rubber surface.

Ink allowed to dry on the blanket surface or a hard glaze of dried gum, ink and paper coating can be removed by washing the surface with a solution of pumice and solvent or pumice and water. A sponge soaked in plain water usually will remove fresh gum streaks from a blanket. Use commercial glaze removers only at infrequent intervals when a pumice washup fails to remove the glaze. To avoid gum glaze formation, wet the blanket surface with plain water before cleaning it with the blanket wash.

One final cleaning tip: Regardless of the type of cleaning solution used, never allow it to stand on the blanket surface longer than necessary. Use two sponges during actual washup procedures. Wet one sponge with the blanket cleaner and immediately after applying the cleaner wipe the blanket surface dry with a sponge or cloth held in the other hand.

Blanket Repair

An offset blanket sometimes sustains serious physical damage during a press run when two or more sheets of paper jam up between the blanket and the impression cylinder. The extra thicknesses of paper mash or compress the fibers in the fabric backing. Such a smash-up creates a low spot in the blanket that results in a light or blank area in the printed image. When this occurs, you may need to remove the blanket and repair the damage.

However, before removing the blanket from the press, place new sheets of packing under it. These will have to be replaced in any case and very often this will prove enough repairwork for smash-ups; the resilient material of modern offset blankets tends to resume its original shape or thickness far better than will any packing sheets, once compressed. Re-secure the blanket and pull an impression with the new packing sheets installed. Chances are the low spot will have disappeared.

If not, prepare the blanket for repair. Depending on the seriousness of the smash-up, four methods of blanket repair offer themselves to the operator.

1. *Water injection:* Less serious dents or low spots in an offset blanket sometimes admit to repair without completely removing the blanket from the press. Release the trailing edge of the blanket and reverse the machine by hand until the damaged area of the fabric backing comes into view. Now inject water into the backing with a hypodermic needle or squeeze water over the compressed fibers from a sponge, thoroughly soaking the damaged area. As the damaged fibers absorb moisture they quickly resume their former size and shape. Warning: if using a hypodermic needle, be extremely careful not to puncture the rubber surface of the blanket; the tiniest hole may admit volatile solvents to the fabric backing during blanket washups.

2. *Paper patch method:* Remove the blanket from the press and build up the low spot with pieces of tissue paper. Cut the tissue patches increasingly larger than the first small piece, which is pasted or glued to the fabric backing at the point of greatest compression. Avoid underlaying the blanket with excessive amounts of tissue patching; it may be necessary to remove the blanket and add or subtract pieces of tissue after pulling an impression. This method often proves tedious, but finds favor with a great many offset press operators.

3. *Blanket massage:* Many offset press operators prefer this method of blanket repair, especially in the case of more serious smash-ups. Merely remove the blanket from the press and roll the damaged area between the palms of both hands. Apply considerable pressure. This heavy massaging of the blanket tends to decompress the individual fibers in the area of damage, allowing them to spring back to their original size and shape.

4. *24-hour soak:* To repair a badly damaged blanket, remove the blanket from the press and immerse it in a pan of water. Be sure to cover the entire blanket with water. Some operators add a wetting agent such as alcohol to the water, theorizing that this encourages a deeper penetration of the fibers. Allow the blanket to soak for 24 hours or longer and then hang it up to dry.

Any of the above methods of blanket repair easily can result in an unacceptably long press downtime. This underscores the necessity of having at least one spare blanket available. Before commencing any extensive blanket repairwork, place a standby blanket on the press and continue the press run.

A smash-up may compress the rubber surface of the blanket as well as its fabric backing. Blanket manufacturers and some lithographic supply houses offer products designed for use on the blanket's rubber surface. Applied as directed to the damaged area, the product causes the rubber surface to swell. Depending on the extent of damage, the amount of impression squeeze and other factors, an application of the rubber swelling material should last from 5,000 to 10,000 impressions. Use no more than specified by the manufacturer to avoid over-swelling the rubber.

Many operators give an offset blanket a 24-hour water soak for reasons other than repairing smash-ups. Over a period of time a blanket's rubber surface may absorb small amounts of ink vehicles or additives, oils or chemicals in the different solvents that come into contact with it. Slow-drying blanket washes are especially prone to deep penetration of the blanket. A gradual, uneven swelling of the blanket occurs, the surface becomes soft and mushy, and reproduction suffers.

In many cases, merely hanging the blanket up in a cool, dry place for two or three days permits the absorbed liquids to evaporate from the rubber surface. Particularly stubborn liquids may require the operator to give the blanket a thorough scrubbing and then immerse it in a pan of water, as described above. After hanging a day or so to dry, the blanket should be ready for use.

Instead of penetrating it, some materials that contact the blanket's surface may form a glaze build-up on the rubber if not removed during washups. This hard glaze limits the ability of the blanket to transfer a full, clear image as the rubber surface loses its original affinity for ink. Surface glaze also can result from exposing the blanket surface for long periods to heaters, radiators or direct sunlight. As suggested earlier, scour the blanket's surface with a pumice and solvent mixture to remove the glaze, and resume proper washup practices to prevent its recurrence.

After a few thousand impressions, a new blanket may suddenly appear to have acquired several low spots or to have diminished appreciably in thickness so that an overall lightening of image occurs for no apparent reason. An operator aiming for a kiss impression is most likely to experience this phenomenon. It does not necessarily mean the blanket has suffered sudden and extensive damage.

Many new blankets lose as much as .003″ in thickness through a normal overall compression of the fabric backing. If this occurs, the best "repairwork" is to place an additional sheet of packing under the entire blanket to bring it again to impression height. Very often a single, full sheet of tissue paper suffices to overcome this normal matting down of the fibers in the fabric backing.

An understanding of the way different physical, mechanical and chemical factors affect the various materials in an offset blanket will better enable the operator to care for the blanket properly and to assess more accurately any damage sustained by it during operation of the press. Proper handling and care as well as sound methods of repairwork will maintain an offset blanket in a near-new condition for many thousands of impressions at the highest standards of lithographic reproduction.

Chapter 8
The Ink and Dampener
Fountain Assemblies

The sheet-fed offset press being a composite of interconnected rollers, gears, cylinders and belts, no part of the machine can claim a greater place of importance than any other part. Nevertheless, since high quality printing by this method of reproduction relies so heavily on a precise and predictable balance of the ink and water distributed along two separate chains of rollers, the two fountain assemblies from which these originate play an extremely vital double role. If either mechanism fails to function properly, the operator immediately loses control over the often delicate ink/water balance. Printing problems of a diverse and serious nature may quickly follow.

In order to avoid these problems and maintain control over the two fountain assemblies, we need an understanding of their mechanical operation, their means of adjustment and especially the cleaning and preventive maintenance procedures recommended for them. Though the ink and water fountains found on most offset presses appear much the same, both in design or appearance and in operation, important differences do exist.

The Ink Fountain

The metal ink fountain resembles a V-shaped trough or pan having a depth and length largely determined by the size of the press. This trough, called "the fountain," holds the supply of ink. A thin metal plate of spring steel called the fountain blade forms the fountain's bottom, or one side of the V. A steel roller, the fountain roller, forms the other side of the V.

As the press runs, the fountain roller turns intermittently while in constant contact with the supply of ink in the fountain. As it turns, the roller picks up a film of ink and transfers an adjustable amount of this film to the metronomic ductor roller. The ductor roller in turn forwards the film of ink to the ink distributing rollers. From here the ink follows the ink form rollers to the plate.

Two things control the amount of ink picked up by the ductor roller: the distance the fountain roller turns while in contact with the ductor roller, and the thickness of the film of ink adhering to the fountain roller as it turns through the supply of ink in the fountain.

The fountain roller turns only a short distance through the supply of ink once each revolution of the press. This distance may vary from a fraction of an inch to a full inch or more, depending on the size of the roller and the turning capacity of the device controlling its movement. The controlling device ordinarily consists of a toothed ratchet and an engaging pawl. The number of ratchet teeth the pawl engages determines the amount or distance the roller turns. The pawl may be set to engage every tooth and turn the roller an extremely short distance or set to engage two or more teeth and turn the roller correspondingly larger distances through the supply of ink. The pawl can also be disengaged entirely to prevent any movement whatsoever of the fountain roller.

Anything that interferes with the free action of the pawl or inhibits the circular movement of the fountain roller will seriously restrict the operator's ability to control the amount of ink entering the inking system.

For the most part, simply keeping the fountain assembly cleaned and oiled insures against malfunction in this area of ink control. Be sure the pawl moves freely on its small shaft. Dirt, grease or dried ink can prevent the pawl from dropping freely and fully between the ratchet teeth. If the pawl hangs up, it may intermittently drop into position behind the wrong tooth. This will alter the ink feed, seriously so on sensitive jobs requiring close control of the ink/water balance. Dirt, grease or dried ink allowed to accumulate in the spaces between the ratchet teeth also may cause the pawl to slip or jump out of the correct notch.

At frequent intervals, thoroughly clean the ratchet and pawl. Use a small, stiff brush soaked with solvent to clean out tiny crevices. Dry both parts and apply a thin film of lightweight oil to the ratchet teeth and to the pawl's shank.

To inspect and clean the fountain roller shaft, it will be necessary to drop or otherwise disengage the fountain blade. Expose the shaft and examine it carefully for dirt or dried ink. The culprit here usually will be dried ink that worked down around the ends of the roller during washup operations. This dried ink may bind the fountain roller and inhibit its movement. More likely, it will prevent full seating of the fountain blade, especially on those presses permitting removal of the fountain blade and its framework for cleaning. In any case, keep the fountain roller shaft clean.

Use a good cleaning solvent and lint-free rags or a brush to remove any encrusted ink. The shank should appear bright and shiny when properly cleaned. A light film of oil may prevent ink from drying so fast to the metal.

The second ink-flow control segment of the ink fountain assembly, the fountain blade, also requires thorough cleaning. Manufacturers have provided for the complete removal of the fountain blades on some presses for ease of cleaning. On other presses, the fountain blade drops back from the fountain roller to expose its forward edge to the cleaning rag.

Clean the fountain blade carefully—front, back and edges—when removing the supply of ink from the fountain. Never allow ink to dry on the fountain blade. Dried ink, or dirt or lint that becomes wedged between the blade and the fountain roller, definitely will prevent fine control of the film of ink fed to the inking rollers. In addition, these foreign particles may become dislodged during operation of the press and cause hickies in a later job.

The operation of the fountain blade controls appears on the surface quite simple. Ink flows from the supply through the gap between the blade's forward edge and the fountain roller. Thumb screws or knobs that fit through the framework under the blade permit the operator to adjust this gap. Turning the adjusting screws in forces the blade closer to the fountain roller and decreases the amount of ink that can flow through the gap. Turning the thumb screws out enlarges the gap and increases the flow of ink.

Actually, the proper operation of these screws proves somewhat more complex than many operators realize. Turning the adjusting screws in a careless, haphazard manner will cause the thin, steel blade to twist and buckle. Not only does this prevent accurate adjustment of the ink flow, it may permanently damage the blade by warping or bending it. Once warped, a fountain blade will stubbornly resist the most painstaking attempts to bring various sections of it into the desired proximity with the fountain roller.

To avoid damage to the fountain blade and correctly adjust the flow of ink past the blade's edge, always start with the center adjusting screw in the line of screws under the fountain. Begin at the center and work out toward both ends, turning one screw at a time. This especially is necessary when tightening the screws, that is moving the fountain blade closer to the fountain roller to decrease the flow of ink. If the operator starts from the center, any wave or buckle that develops in the blade will be "ironed out" harmlessly toward the ends of the blade as each screw is drawn tighter in turn. To do otherwise risks trapping a wave somewhere in the middle of the blade between two of the thumb screws. This wave permits excess flow of ink; it may become permanently set in the thin metal.

The operator must also avoid drawing any of the adjusting screws so tightly against the fountain blade that the blade rubs against the fountain roller. This will result in a wearing of the roller or the blade or both. Excessively tightened screws may cause the blade to score the turning fountain roller. Over a long period of time, excessive screw pressure will result in a wearing of the blade's edge which will take on a scalloped appearance. You will find it nearly impossible to adjust the flow of ink satisfactorily with a blade having a badly scalloped edge.

Stripped threads or impacted dirt or dried ink that prevents the adjusting screws from turning freely may lead to inadvertently overtightening the screws. The screws must move freely enough that the resistance of the fountain blade can be felt as the screws tighten down against it. Periodically, or as inspection shows a need for it, turn the screws all the way out to clean and oil them and the holes in which they fit. To avoid damaging either the blade or the threads of the adjusting screws, it is a good idea to back off the screws a full turn before removing the fountain blade from the press or from its metal frame to clean it.

Operated correctly and with all its moving parts kept cleaned, oiled and free from damage, the ink fountain assembly will provide years of trouble-free ink-flow control.

Press view showing general relationship of ink assembly to rollers and plate.

The Dampening or Water Fountain

Offset printing depends upon the controlled marriage or blending of a thin film of lithographic ink with an equally thin film of carefully prepared fountain solution. The dampening solution, primarily water in content, feeds into the dampening system from a pan or fountain that normally holds a specific amount of the solution. By following a system of periodic cleaning and maintenance, the operator insures continued trouble-free operation of the water fountain assembly.

All moving parts of the water fountain benefit from a regular program of cleaning and oiling. During operation of the press and during washup procedures, ink often works back through the chain of dampening rollers to the water fountain. Clean this ink as well as any gum, dirt, lint or other foreign matter from the fountain and from the fountain roller.

Ink or gum may bind the fountain roller and inhibit its movement. Any greasy or gummy material on the surface of the fountain roller tends to render it hydrophobic. A hydrophobic fountain roller rejects moisture. The fountain roller must turn freely at all times and its surface must remain hydrophilic, or water-loving, in order for it to function properly.

The operator should periodically clean the fountain, preferably at the end of each shift of work. Remove all the old fountain solution and rinse or flush the fountain with clear water. Mop up any excess water with a sponge. Use a lint-free rag or small brush soaked in a good cleaning solvent to clean away any dried ink, gum or dirt from the device that controls the movement of the fountain roller. Lightly oil the fountain roller shank or spindles as well as the controlling ratchet and pawl.

The metal water fountain roller on an offset press will benefit immeasurably from a systematic cleaning operation designed to renew its water receptivity. Once a week or oftener the operator should:

1. Go over the entire roller surface with a good grade of scratch remover or manufacturer-recommended fountain roller cleaner. This cleans the metal of any residue of ink and gum without damaging the roller surface. Rinse away the scratch remover with plain water.

2. Apply a film of concentrated fountain etch to the roller.

3. Immediately after applying the etch, go over the roller with a pad moistened with alcohol. Alcohol halts the action of the etch and dries the roller's surface.

4. Finally, apply a film of gum arabic to the roller and rub it dry with cheesecloth or other lint-free material.

This simple four-step cleaning, etching and gumming operation returns the fountain roller to its original hydrophilic (water-loving) condition. In place of scratch remover in the first step, many operators dip a molleton pad in water then in fine pumice powder and scrub down the roller's surface with this lightly abrasive cleaner. However, technicians recommend this procedure only on those presses where the fountain roller can be removed from the machine for cleaning. Otherwise, pumice powder particles will collect in the fountain and eventually work forward through the dampening system to wear the plate, blanket and inking roller surfaces during operation of the press.

An alternative to the above procedure that takes less time involves coating the cleaned roller with a 50/50 mixture of fountain solution concentrate and 14° Baume gum. Use scratch remover or pumice powder to clean the roller, rinse the surface with clear water, then wipe on the concentrate/gum mixture. Wipe the roller dry with cheesecloth.

One or the other of the above cleaning procedures is also recommended for the metal distributing or vibrator roller in the dampening system. The operator will want this roller kept in a water-receptive condition also.

With the water fountain assembly cleaned, oiled and in good working condition, it should deliver easily controlled amounts of water to the system of molleton- or paper-covered dampener rollers. Two things control the amount of solution extracted from the water pan by the fountain roller: the distance the roller travels through the supply of water during each revolution of the press and the length of time the ductor rests or dwells against the fountain roller.

On many presses the fountain roller turns slowly on its shaft at speeds that vary with the speed of the press. On smaller presses, a ratchet-and-pawl device similar to that which controls the ink fountain roller turns the water fountain roller a short distance through the supply of solution each revolution of the press. Newer, larger

Dampening solution mounted on small press.

presses have an independent, variable-speed drive connected to the water fountain roller. This permits fine adjustment to the speed of the constantly turning roller. As its turning speed or its distance of travel increases, the fountain roller lifts more water from the pan. Decreasing the speed or distance of travel decreases the amount of water picked up.

The dwell, or length of time the metronomic ductor roller remains in contact with the turning fountain roller, also controls the amount of water fed to the dampening system. The longer the ductor remains in contact with the turning fountain roller, the more water it picks up. The shorter the dwell, the less moisture passes from fountain roller to ductor roller.

To control the amount of water traveling through the dampening system, then, carefully adjust the speed or distance of fountain roller turn or the dwell of the ductor roller, or both.

On forms requiring considerably less water over some areas of the image, the operator utilizes another means of controlling the amount of water. Rubber water stops of various design are affixed to the fountain on most presses. When in direct contact with the turning fountain roller these water stops decrease the amount of moisture delivered to the ductor roller. They do this by stripping off some of the fountain solution picked up by the fountain roller and permitting it to drain back into the pan. Adjust these rubber stops with care—some of them have metal clamps that can deeply score the fountain roller surface.

Proper operation of the two fountain assemblies, combined with a regular program of inspection, cleaning and oiling of all their moving parts, definitely prove their value in permitting you to more easily control the ink/water balance while running the press.

Chapter 9
The Rollers on an
Offset Press

The operator of an offset press must cope with two banks or sets of rollers, often referred to as roller "chains." These two roller systems have separate but equally important functions. One chain of rollers, the inking rollers, delivers ink to the plate's image areas. At the same time, the other chain of rollers, the dampening rollers, forwards a film of moisture, the fountain solution, to the plate's non-image areas.

The offset press operator aware of the importance to high quality presswork of sustaining an ink-and-water balance correct for the job being run, realizes the necessity for systematically following a program of roller inspection, roller cleaning, roller storage and roller reconditioning or replacement.

The Inking Rollers

The ink distribution system on offset presses commonly utilizes two types of rollers—hard rollers, usually made of steel, and soft resilient rubber or composition (synthetic) rollers.* Either type of roller can present the operator with ink distribution difficulties of a serious nature.

The two problems most commonly associated with metal inking rollers, stripping and corrosion, result in an inability of these rollers to carry an even film of ink. A "stripped" roller may refuse to carry any ink at all in a narrow band around its circumference. Ink

---

*We also may find inking rollers of plastic, nylon, Teflon and of other new or experimental materials designed to resist the effects of gums, acids and strong washup solutions that come in contact with them.

appears to have been physically stripped from the roller. Actually, the roller surface in the area of the bared band has rejected the ink molecules forwarded to it from the preceding roller or rollers.

Several factors can lead to metal roller stripping. Excess gum or acid in the fountain solution, extremely thin films of ink that cause repeated heavy wear on the roller surfaces, incorrect roller settings, too much drier in the ink, a poorly desensitized plate or improper washup procedures — any one of these or a combination can lead to roller stripping. A visual inspection of metal inking rollers during operation of the press usually reveals a stripping condition to the operator.

A closer examination of the rollers after press washup, however, is required to detect corrosion on the roller surfaces. Corrosion, usually caused by continued neglect, will appear spottily, at irregular intervals across the roller. Ink will not adhere properly to these corroded areas.

Occasionally, the operator can overcome a not-too-serious stripping condition by dressing down the affected metal roller surface with pumice powder. Clean the press in the usual manner, then remove the rubber intermediate and form inking rollers from the press, as well as the important metal oscillating or vibrator rollers the machine may carry. This permits work on the metal rollers without interference and makes it easier to remove all traces of pumice powder.

With the metal rollers clean and bare of ink, press a rag dampened with cleaning solvent in a mound of finely ground pumice. Go over the entire surface of each metal inking roller on the press, then wipe away all traces of the pumice powder. Treat the small metal oscillating rollers in the same manner.

If stripping persists, we must take stronger measures to combat it. Many lithographic supply houses offer a special copperplating solution that, when applied as directed, returns metal rollers to their original ink-loving condition. Copperplating a metal roller combats both stripping and corrosion by overlaying the impaired roller surface with a coating of copper, a material that has a greater affinity for ink than does steel.

With most copperplating solutions the operator can either coat the cleaned metal rollers manually with a cloth or sponge soaked in the solution or pour the mixture across the top roller in the inking system and allow it to distribute as the press turns over at slow speed. Follow the directions supplied by the manufacturer. Technicians recommend rinsing the plated rollers with an alcohol wash, using isopropyl alcohol.

Many offset press operators prefer to work with a non-proprietary copperplating solution. A popular formula is comprised of the following ingredients:

Isopropyl Alcohol (99% Grade) . . . . 34 liq. oz.
Ethylene Glycol . . . . 34 liq. oz.
Hydrochloric Acid (37%-38%) . . . . 3¼ liq. oz.
Cuprous Chloride . . . . 2¼ Av. oz.

Mix the ingredients together in the order listed. Powdered cuprous chloride ($CU_2 CL_2$) will refuse to go into solution properly if added ahead of the acid.

It must be noted that this wipe-on method of copperplating metal inking rollers is not permanent. Friction between the metal roller and the adjacent rubber rollers quickly wears away the thin copper coating. It may wear away in from one week to six months. To avoid a resumption of stripping problems the operator will have to reapply the copperizing solution at more or less frequent intervals.

A more permanent method of copperplating metal rollers involves removing the rollers from the press and having them factory coated electrolytically. Electroplated rollers retain their copper coating indefinitely, provided the use of strong acids or harsh abrasives on them is avoided. Manufacturers now electroplate the metal inking rollers on many presses at the factory to prevent stripping.

The rubber inking rollers on an offset press also may lose their affinity for ink and strip. The stripping may occur in a narrow band around the roller or at irregular intervals across the roller. As when the metal rollers strip, this condition on the rubber inking rollers results in poor distribution of the ink and in a lowering of printing quality.

Prevention is the best cure for rubber roller stripping. For the most part, prevention involves nothing more complex than adhering to a systematic program of roller washup. Nothing leads to

stripping of rubber inking rollers quicker than poor washup practices, though other factors also may contribute to the condition.
Inadequate washups quickly lead to other problems, too, such as
roller cracking and distortion of roller circumference.

Cleaning the rollers on a press having an automatic washup
device presents no problems so long as recommended cleaning
solvents are used and the washup device is kept in good operating
condition. Keep the rubber, plastic or nylon blade of the washup
device adjusted so that, when engaged, it just touches the contacting roller's surface, across the entire length of the roller.
Periodically examine the blade's forward or cleaning edge for nicks,
breaks or worn spots. The operator can true up some of these blades
with a small file or with fine sandpaper carefully drawn across the
blade at its original cleaning angle. Replace a badly worn or
damaged blade to insure good roller cleaning. On small presses
lacking a washup device, remove the rollers from the press rather
than attempt to leave them in place for final cleaning operations.

The type of cleaning solvent used has much to do not only with
how clean the rollers get but with the state of their physical condition. To minimize hardening of their surfaces, wash the rollers
with a bland solution before the ink dries rather than at less frequent intervals with a strong or harsh washup solution. Many
operators use naphtha or a similar petroleum distillate. However,
these operators periodically follow a double application of naphtha
with a vigorous pumice powder rubdown of the rollers to insure a
thorough cleaning of their surfaces.

Offset press technicians generally recommend the use of one of
the newer two-step or three-step cleaners, especially on presses
equipped with an automatic washup device. Used as directed, these
special cleaning solvents lift ink from the roller surfaces with far
greater efficiency than the naphtha or kerosene solutions still used
in some plants. This, of course, goes far toward preventing any
buildup of dried-ink glaze and the problems associated with this
condition.

The operator applies a two- or three-step cleaner to the rollers
in a particular sequence while running the press at slow speed. In
the case of a two-step cleaner, the first solvent lifts all, or most, of
the ink from the rollers. The second solvent then removes any ink

left by the first solvent and, in addition, removes all traces of the first solvent from the rollers and leaves them clean and dry.

A three-step cleaner works much in the same manner with the exception that the first of the three solvents acts primarily as a catalytic agent. It effectively dislodges all the pigment particles of the ink from the roller surfaces and holds them in suspension until the second solvent reaches the rollers.

Observe carefully the efficacy of cleaning operations no matter which type of cleaner or method of washup utilized. It may be necessary to hand clean the rollers' ends after each washup in order to prevent a buildup of dried ink here. All rubber inking rollers also will benefit from a periodic rubdown with pumice powder.

For this operation, remove the rollers from the press to avoid diffusing abrasive pumice powder particles through the machine. Many operators use a solution of naphtha and pumice to clean the rollers, and this works well in most cases. However, plain water best removes that part of roller glaze formed by dried gum. Soak a rag in solvent or water then press it into a mound of pumice powder. Enough powder will adhere to the rag to permit easy cleaning of the roller. The rag should contain enough moisture to turn the pumice into a medium thick paste. Rub the rag back and forth over the roller's entire surface, applying considerable pressure so the slightly abrasive pumice particles will lift dried ink and gum from the roller. To insure against transporting particles to the press, place the cleaned roller in a sink and thoroughly flush its surface with running water.

Any system of roller cleaning should have one goal: renewing the rubber surface of each roller to its original velvety textured, ink-loving condition. Rollers subjected to the daily stresses of acids, oils, varnishes, solvents, dirt and abrasives require regular washups. Beyond this, the importance of a regular cleaning program lies partly in the fact that it forces the operator to remain aware of the condition of all the inking rollers.

Roller deterioration often occurs slowly over a period of months or even years. Without remaining continually aware of their condition, we may fail to observe the gradual loss of printing quality until one or more of the rollers begin to strip, break up or cause other serious printing problems. The seriousness of observed

Rollers should be immediately replaced whenever deterioration becomes visible to the eye.

roller deterioration will determine whether the roller should be replaced or factory reground or if a vigorous scrubbing of the roller will renew its glazed surface to the desired printing quality.

In addition to proper cleaning practices, be sure to give special attention to the storage of spare rollers. Though synthetic rubber rollers generally hold up well in storage, they may harden or become distorted if stored for a long time. Direct sunlight tends to oxidize the surface of rubber rollers, which should be stored in a dark area away from sources of high heat. In storage, prevent surface-to-surface contact of the rollers; prolonged pressure may permanently distort the rubber surface. If possible, store synthetic rubber rollers so the roller shafts support their entire weight. Periodically turn all the rollers stored in a rack to prevent any sagging of the rubber material.

Combining spare roller care with a systematic program of roller washup can keep the inking rollers on an offset press functioning satisfactorily and in a like-new condition for a surprisingly long time.

The Dampening Rollers

Generally fewer in number than the inking rollers, the dampening rollers on an offset press deserve equal care and attention. Unless these rollers are kept in good operating condition, maintaining a proper ink/water balance during a press run will prove difficult, if not impossible.

As with the inking system, the dampening system on most sheet-fed offset presses utilizes two types of rollers—hard rollers and soft rollers. The hard dampening rollers commonly have a water-loving metal surface, either aluminum or chromium. The soft rollers in the dampening system on most presses consist of a metal core or shaft covered with rubber to a specified depth and hardness.

One or more layers of absorbent cotton material, usually supplied by manufacturers in tubular form for easy installation, cover the metal-and-rubber core of the soft rollers. The outer layer likely will be one of the deep-nap molleton covers. Many operators use paper covers on form dampening rollers. The paper cover may come in tubular or sleeve form or in the less expensive roll form which the operator wraps around the roller in overlapping bands from one end of the roller to the other.

Dampening roller maintenance begins with a close inspection of the various rollers in the system, with particular attention directed toward the condition of the roller coverings. Dampening rollers require covers both clean and free of tears, gouges or excessively worn spots. In most cases, periodic visual inspection of the rollers will suffice to detect severe physical defects of the covering material as well as reveal high levels of accumulated ink. If printing problems such as mourning band scum,* roller stripping or excessive plate wear persist though the dampening rollers appear in perfect condition, a check of the rollers' pressure settings with strips of paper or thin plastic may reveal out-of-round roller stock or a lumpy, uneven covering.

Because adequate control of the moisture supplied to the plate requires that each water roller lie perfectly parallel with the other rollers in the dampening system, and with the plate cylinder, the operator should replace an out-of-round or warped roller with a new roller at once. No amount of recovering or adjusting will overcome so serious a defect in a dampening roller. Attempting to compensate for a warped roller only serves to hasten the wear to other parts of the dampening system or to the plate.

Fortunately, when the operator handles the rollers with care, serious damage to the roller stock occurs only infrequently. For the most part, apparent unevenness of a dampening roller results from worn, baggy or improperly installed covers. Renewing the roller to its original uniform roundness requires merely replacing one or more layers of the covering material. The sudden appearance of a printing problem usually indicates to the alert operator the need for a new dampening roller cover.

Under normal operating conditions, the ductor roller may require recovering more frequently than the other rollers in the dampening system. The ductor roller's metronomic action swings it into sharp, repeated contact with the fountain roller and the metal vibrator roller. The ductor roller continually stops and starts

---

This condition derives its name from dark bands that appear along the right and left sides of the printed sheet when non-image areas on the plate near its outside edges become ink-receptive, and print.

throughout the press run. This causes severe friction and considerable wear to the cover. As a consequence, this important roller should be inspected more frequently than the other rollers to be sure it carries an adequate and even film of moisture from one end to the other. Dampening, good or poor, begins with the operation of the ductor roller.

Most offset press operators cover the ductor roller with a tubular type of molleton covering material. With practice, anyone having a reasonable degree of manual dexterity can quickly and correctly install a tubular or sleeve molleton cover on a dampening roller.

From the supply of cover material cut a piece slightly longer than the roller to be covered. Pull this sleeve smoothly onto the roller. On larger presses, use the metal cylinder provided for easy installation. Approximately 1/2 " of the molleton sleeve should extend beyond either end of the roller. Using a strong thread or cord, stitch these overlaps in a manner that they can be drawn down tightly over the roller ends. Tie off the end of each cord so it does not slip and allow the cover to slide back from the ends of the roller.

The form dampening rollers also require recovering from time to time, as inspection of the rollers or a decrease in the quality of printing dictates. Each form dampening roller often will have two or more layers of cloth covering material. The underlayers act as a water reservoir to insure that an even supply of moisture remains available to the top layer and subsequently to the plate. At infrequent intervals it will be necessary to replace all the layers of covering material. Usually, only the top layer will need replacing. Each layer of cover material will have a different weave or texture; do not place an inner-layer cover on the outside or vice versa.

Where the top layer is of the cloth or molleton variety, replacement follows much the same procedure as outlined for the ductor roller. Be sure the heavy, water-trapping nap of the cover faces outward as installed on the roller. Molleton covering material usually must be turned inside out during installation, with the aid of the metal cylinder. Smooth the molleton onto the roller and tie the ends securely in place.

Many operators prefer the newer paper dampener covers. This cover, made of high wet-strength paper, absorbs very little water, but immediately transfers its supply of moisture to the plate. This theoretically makes possible instantaneous adjustments to the amount of moisture delivered to the plate. Manufacturers provide these covers in tube form, cut to size for the press in use. The paper dampener cover or sleeve slips easily onto the roller then, when moistened, shrinks to conform to the circumference of the roller. The pre-cut paper sleeve eliminates sewing operations. A significant difference between paper sleeves and molleton covers is that the former fit onto specially made rubber rollers rather than over layers of cloth covering material.

Less expensive 2½ " to 3 " wide rolls of parchment-like paper also provide dampener covering material in many print shops. Installation here requires somewhat more skill. Starting at one end of the roller, wind the pre-wet paper in overlapping bands the entire length of the roller. Take considerable care in maintaining an even overlap—usually of about 1/4"—and in preventing the development of wrinkles in the paper. The ends of the wrap are secured by rubber bands or lengths of string looped once around the ends of the roller, directly over shallow grooves in the rubber at each end.

Offset press technicians recommend cleaning the dampening rollers at the end of each shift of operation. The operator also should thoroughly clean the dampening rollers when changing from one color of ink to another, especially when going to a lighter color. Regular cleaning of dampening rollers is of great importance to good quality presswork.

Some large printing plants have automatic dampening roller cleaning devices for cloth- or molleton-covered rollers. The dampeners to be cleaned ride on motor driven stainless steel rollers in a trough or tub. To operate, run enough water into the tub to partly cover the rollers, then add an amount of ink dissolving solvent, preferably one recommended by the roller manufacturer. The solvent used should be of a type that will evaporate quickly from the cover material.

The motor driven metal roller turns the rollers rapidly through the cleaning mixture of water and solvent. When this action has cleaned the ink from the rollers, drain the tub and flush the still turning rollers with clear water. On most such cleaning devices, another motor driven roller permits rapid spin-drying of the cleaned and rinsed dampening rollers. Where ink has heavily saturated the dampening roller covers, initially apply a liberal amount of the recommended cleaning solvent to the rollers before applying the water bath in order to loosen the ink.

In smaller plants, the operator will have to hand clean the dampening rollers. This should not prove a difficult task so long as cleaning occurs before any ink has dried on the rollers. Fast drying inks may require mid-day cleaning of the dampening rollers, or whenever the press will remain idle as during lunch hour periods.

Dampener covers or sleeves can slip on rollers.

To hand clean a molleton-covered dampening roller, place the roller in a sink or tub of hot water. Use a stiff bristled brush and briskly scrub the entire surface of the roller. Apply the recommended cleaning solvent as needed. Some technicians recommend thoroughly scrubbing a gum arabic solution into the dampener cover before applying solvent or water to the roller. When the solvent has lifted all, or most, of the ink from the roller, flush the entire roller surface with clean, warm water. Be sure to remove all traces of the solvent and loosened ink. Use a blunt knife or heavy rubber blade to squeegee excess water from the roller.

Although the inexpensive roll paper dampener covering material is designed to be discarded when it becomes dirtied, many operators carefully hand wash the cover with a suitable solvent at the end of each shift of work. This significantly increases the life of a wrapped paper cover. Paper dampener sleeves also should be cleaned by hand. Wipe the entire surface of the roller with a lint-free rag soaked in a manufacturer-recommended solvent; a quick-drying, non-oily press wash or plate cleaner should enable the operator to remove the film of ink deposited on a paper sleeve without harming the cover material.

Properly cleaned, dampener roller covers, of cotton or of paper, provide uniform moisture distribution over an extended period of time before replacement becomes necessary. Dampener roller cover replacement remains largely dependent upon two factors: visual inspection of the covers and the quality of reproduction obtained with the press. Dampening roller maintenance—cover cleaning and cover replacement—provides the most important means available to the operator for sustained top performance of the dampening system on an offset press.

Chapter 10
Preventing
Plate Problems

A number of the printing problems encountered by an offset press operator stem from faulty platemaking, plate handling or related procedures. The most skillful platemaker occasionally produces a plate that refuses to perform as desired. An inexperienced platemaker may produce several plates that fail to perform satisfactorily. The operator who doubles as platemaker in a small printing plant inadvertently may create many plate-related problems, perhaps by incorrectly applying developing fluids to unfamiliar plates. If either the platemaker or the operator mishandles one of the thin, light-sensitive paper or metal plates, before or after it reaches the press, the incurred damage easily can render the plate useless.

Offset plate imperfections that arise from improper plate processing or plate handling procedures often fail to manifest themselves until after the operator has installed the plate on the press and commenced makeready tasks. Like many other printing problems, plate-related difficulties may have more than a single contributory cause.

The operator who learns to recognize those problems most likely to have originated with platemaking or plate handling operations will waste little time at the press attempting to correct a difficulty that eventually will require the platemaker to rework the defective plate or produce a new plate. Plate-related press problems generally fall into two classifications, those arising from plate processing errors and those that develop from plate handling errors.

Plate Processing Errors

Blind Plate Image: Blinding occurs when the image, or small affected areas of the image, refuse to accept ink. Light, uninked streaks often appear in the print. In their configuration, they may resemble streaks left on a wet window by a sponge or squeegee that fails to remove all the water from the glass. This type of plate blinding normally becomes noticeable during the initial rollup of the plate, in the early stages of press makeready.

A common cause of plate blinding—heavy, streaked films of gum arabic adhering to an image area of the plate—usually indicates a failure to remove all the excess gum from the plate during platemaking operations. The protective gum coat should be polished to a thin, dry film, preferably with a clean pad of cheesecloth. Some plates blind extensively if the platemaker uses a gum arabic other than the preparation specified by and obtainable from the manufacturer of the plate. This especially may be true in the case of subtractive plates. These plates require a special "subtractive gum" to finish them properly. Chemical contamination also can cause plate blinding by affecting one or more of the steps of plate processing. Handle and process all offset plates in a clean area free of contaminates to prevent this.

Normally the operator will not have to request a new plate when blinding appears. One of the following procedures usually will correct the condition.

1. Thoroughly wash the entire plate with warm water to remove excess gum from its surface.

2. Run from 50 to 100 waste sheets through the press with the impression on, but with the form inking and dampening rollers in the "off" position. The waste sheets should wear away any film or streaks of gum and leave all image areas ink receptive.

3. Rub down the plate with undiluted fountain solution concentrate or apply a 10%-15% solution of phosphoric acid to the plate with a pad of cheesecloth.

4. Go over the plate with a rag or sponge soaked in an image activator, plate cleaner or image lacquer and immediately roll up the plate. Use the activator, cleaner or lacquer recommended and specially formulated for the plate in use.

If plate blinding develops after the press run has actually commenced, the operator probably should suspect as the causative factor some area of press makeready or preparation. For instance, if the inking rollers fail to forward enough ink to the plate or if insufficient amounts of ink transfer from plate to blanket surface during each revolution of the press, a defect resembling plate blinding eventually will appear in the printed image. Examine the surface condition of the rubber blanket and all the rollers in the inking system. Make sure these surfaces are fully capable of accepting and transferring an adequate film of ink.

Other things to check include the fountain solution, which may contain excessive amounts of gum arabic, have a high concentration of acid (indicated by a reading below 3.5 on the pH scale) or contain alcohol in excess of 30 percent; the ink, which may have too much drier, have insufficient tack or lack good flowing properties (a short ink); and the fountain rollers, which may have retained some of the detergent used in cleaning them. Examine and correct these areas if necessary before returning a blinded plate to the platemaker for reprocessing or replacement.

Dot Gain or Dot Loss: During a pre-makeready examination of halftone areas on a plate with the microscope, the operator may discover the individual dots that make up the image have a different size than corresponding dots in the negative. The dots on the plate may appear larger or they may appear smaller. In an extreme case some halftone dots will disappear altogether from the plate.

Obviously, such a plate cannot provide a faithful reproduction of the original copy. To insure precision printing, the operator will have to obtain a new plate, one bearing same-size halftone dots. An understanding of some of the more common causes of dot gain or loss will help beginning platemakers as well as those operators who process their own plates.

Dot gain or loss often results from improper exposure of the plate. If the platemaker relies on an old, yellowed gray scale, exposure time probably will not be correct for any of the plates processed. A malfunctioning timing device also could lead to underexposing or overexposing offset plates. Moving the light source closer to or further from the vacuum frame without initiating a corresponding decrease or increase in exposure time also will cause halftone dots to enlarge or to shrink in size.

Poor contact between the negative and the plate, caused by hard foreign particles lodged between the two, by air trapped between plate and film or by insufficient evacuation of air from the vacuum frame, encourages dot gain. Poor negative-to-plate contact causes the dots to spread or gain in size because light can strike a larger area of the plate as it passes through the openings in the negative. The wider the space between film and plate, the larger the circumference of each affected halftone dot.

A seemingly mysterious dot loss sometimes will occur even though the platemaker uses the correct exposure time and carefully follows the recommended developing and gumming procedures, but has used an old, yellowed negative during exposure. In this case a dot size discrepancy may become apparent only through a detailed comparison of previously printed sheets with a new print. It will be necessary to procure a new negative having fully open holes and to expose and develop a new plate.

Depending upon the type of plate in use, either overdeveloping or underdeveloping the image can cause a dot gain or a dot loss. To avoid this problem as well as several others, always develop an exposed plate exactly as recommended by its manufacturer, using clean pads and fresh developing fluids kept within temperature ranges deemed best for each preparation. Improper development of a plate frequently can be corrected by redeveloping it, while holding strictly to the proper plate processing procedures.

Before changing any platemaking procedure, equipment or material to overcome a dot gain or loss problem, double-check the manufacturer's recommendations to determine the correct exposure time and proper developing procedures for the plate in use. Remember that some plates experience dot gain through overexposure or overdevelopment while dot gain occurs on other plates if they receive too little exposure or insufficient development. If in doubt, refer to the manufacturer's platemaking guide or contact the manufacturer direct to learn which reaction to expect from too much or too little exposure or development.

Halation: Offset technicians use the term halation when speaking of the effect on the plate image of a negative that does not fully contact all areas of the plate during exposure. An out-of-contact negative allows extra light to pass through the holes in the negative and strike the plate at an angle. This causes an enlargement of the halftone dots — dot gain. (In the case of positive acting plates, halation causes dot loss.)

Usually, the press operator observes halation in the form of a heavier, darker band in the printed image around halftone areas. The enlarged dots visibly cover a larger percentage of the printed sheet than they should. Occasionally, those darker areas appear somewhere in the center of a halftone.

A halation problem often signifies an error made in the stripping department, where negatives are affixed to goldenrod masking sheets or flats preparatory to exposure of the press plate. To prevent halation, strippers should:

— —Examine films, flats and work areas for dirt. Always prepare goldenrod flats on a clean surface and use cleaned tools. Particles of dirt clinging to the film, the flat or to stripping tape often create the conditions that give rise to halation problems.

— —Never construct a flat or masking sheet of material over .004" thick. If the goldenrod exceeds .004", its edges can press against the plate heavily enough during exposure to create an out-of-contact space between negative and plate.

— —Leave at least ¼" of border around each halftone image area when trimming negatives to be secured to a flat. This permits placement of stripping tape well back from the edges of a halftone. Tape placed closer to a halftone than ¼" may cause a loss of negative-to-plate contact.

— —Avoid the use of films having different thicknesses. Placing a thick negative next to a thinner negative encourages halation.

— —Avoid overlapping films in a flat. Butt them together and use thin strips of masking tape to bind their edges. Overlapped films cause halation difficulties by creating an out-of-contact condition.

When halation causes a plate defect that appears in the print as a visible dark band outlining a halftone or as darkened spots within a halftone area, the operator has no choice but to request a replacement plate. Once exposed to an abnormally large size on a plate, halftone dots cannot be shrunk to proper dimensions by reworking the plate.

Image Loss: Extensive image loss attributable to faulty platemaking usually indicates an underexposure of the plate. The press operator probably will not see the plate; the defect being readily apparent, the platemaker will expose a new plate. Image loss may or may not be confined to halftones. Other image areas also can experience a weakening or loss.

An image loss the operator may encounter is that resulting from water contacting the plate prior to exposure. A loss of image caused by water droplets usually effects only small areas of the image and thus may escape detection in the plateroom. The operator frequently can repair small broken images in solid areas with an image touch-up fluid available from the plate manufacturer. More extensive areas of image loss require the production of a new plate. Some types of plates cannot tolerate moisture at any time, during or after exposure or development.

Poor plate gumming also can lead to image loss. Here, the broken images may appear spotty or streaked in small areas of the image or image loss may affect relatively large areas of the plate. Always use sufficient gum arabic after plate development and polish it smooth to a thin, dry film.

Opaquing fluid allowed to dry on the negative can cause a complete image loss of any area covered. Masking paper or an opaque tape that covers any image area will have the same effect. Examine all image areas of a negative (and background areas of a positive) before placing plate and flat in the vacuum frame.

Plugging: In plate plugging, ink molecules have a tendency to cling to small non-image areas of a halftone. As the ink builds up, these areas begin to print. A close examination may reveal even the microscopic areas between halftone dots have plugged, or filled in with ink. Fine type or small reverses often fill in if plugging develops. Plugging usually affects unpatterned, perhaps widely scattered areas of the plate.

Since too much ink, an ink that's either too tacky or too soupy, dirty dampeners, a lumpy-surfaced or embossed blanket, incorrect cylinder or form inking roller pressure settings, an improperly formulated fountain solution or uncoated paper stock can also cause a filling in of halftones or fine print, the operator should carefully examine these before requesting the platemaker to rework the plate or make a new one. The platemaker usually can correct a plugged plate by properly redeveloping it. Platemakers avoid plugging that originates with plate processing procedures by:

— —Keeping the work area and all plate processing tools clean.

— —Rinsing old developer from new sponges and discarding old, worn sponges.

— —Exposing each plate as recommended by its manufacturer. (Plugging that develops from incorrect plate exposure will mean making a new plate.)

— —Developing all plates at the correct temperatures, especially avoiding the use of warm chemicals. (Unless otherwise specified, maintain chemical and developing sink temperatures below 80° F.)

— —Using fresh chemicals kept tightly capped and sealed in their original containers.

Scumming: Scumming describes the effect on the printed image when non-image areas of a plate become sensitized and begin to carry ink. The print appears smudged or dirtied. Scumming can occur in small spots over wide areas of the plate or in narrow bands across the plate or in bands the full length of the plate, around the plate cylinder.

Incorrectly adjusted form dampening or inking rollers, excessive printing pressures, chemicals from the paper being run as well as certain ink formulas can cause or aggravate a scumming situation. All these areas should be checked when a plate scums.

A few causes of plate scum originate in the platemaking department. Incomplete or incorrect plate processing may, of course, bring about the condition. Especially with new or unfamiliar plates, follow plate processing instructions exactly as written, and use only those chemicals prescribed.

A hard-to-develop plate may forewarn of scumming difficulties; it also may indicate an unintentional or partial exposure of some non-image areas of the plate. Partial exposure of a non-image area definitely will cause a plate to scum. A possible cause of non-image exposure can be a negative not completely opaque in the affected areas or the use of masking paper not sufficiently opaque to shield these areas from the exposure light. An extremely thin coating of gum arabic also can permit scumming to develop if the gum wears away during the early part of the press run. Use a full-strength gum preparation not diluted by too much water and polish it to a thin, dry coat on the plate.

One unusual cause of plate scum that originates in the stripping department, may occur only infrequently, making its cause difficult to pinpoint. If the stripper uses cellophane masking tape, scum can develop wherever the tape contacts a non-image area of the plate. This happens because cellophane backed tape tends to absorb moisture, and the moisture then sensitizes the small surface area of the plate on which the tape may rest for any prolonged period of time. Tape scum usually can be recognized by its location on the plate and by the size and shape of the scum. To avoid the problem, use only tapes having an acetate or plastic base especially manufactured for the lithographic industry.

Plate Handling Errors

Plate handling equals plate processing practices in importance, though instances of defective plates caused by the former may be fewer in number. A defective plate needs reconditioning or replacement whatever the cause.

Some plate-related problems caused by improper handling may at first inspection appear to have developed from faulty platemaking activities.

Plugging, where scattered non-image areas of a halftone fill in, and scumming provide two such examples. Either of these problems will develop if a heavy enough concentration of stray light strikes the plate prior to its exposure in the vacuum frame. The light can come from any source. Its effect on the plate results in a partial exposure in spots or streaks across the plate. Both the platemaker and the press operator may blame or suspect all the causes listed under "Plate Processing Errors" before suspecting stray light exposure for the difficulty.

To avoid accidental exposure of a plate, or any portion of it, handle unexposed offset plates only under yellow light. Yellow light lacks the plate-activating ultraviolet rays of ordinary lighting, yet provides sufficient illumination to work under. A plateroom lighting system that permits a quick switchover from regular white lighting to yellow lighting and back again will prove a worthwhile investment in any plant striving for top quality reproductions. Regular lighting has an insignificant effect on exposed and fully processed offset plates.

Unexposed plates also require a reliable means of safe storage. Give them the same respect and care unexposed sheets of any photographic film or paper would receive. Store packaged plates flat and arrange multiple packages so the oldest plates rest on top. Most plate manufacturers stamp each package with an expiration date to prevent overlong storage of unprocessed plates. Keep opened and unopened packages of offset plates in a cool, dry place away from any source of moisture or heat such as a sink or an electric heater. Permitting moisture in any form to reach unexposed offset plates can result in a loss of image similar to that caused by underexposure. Water splashed from a sink directly onto the packages or moisture condensing from a humid atmosphere can cause image loss difficulties.

Offset plates come from the factory carefully packaged in material designed to protect them from unwanted light and moisture as well as dirt, dust and other forms of contamination. Examine each package for tears and holes. Cover any openings with strips of opaque tape to prevent any leakage of light into the package. Most manufacturers have each package constructed with interlocking flaps so that once opened it can be closed again when a plate has been removed. To further protect the plates from dust and dirt, from scratches and other accidents, the manufacturer usually places a thin sheet of non-absorbent paper between the plates in a package. Many platemakers find it advisable to leave this slipsheet on the top plate in the package when removing a plate. Of course, the package should be completely closed before storage.

Offset plates require care in handling to prevent surface scratches or accidental bending. Avoid sliding a plate out of a package. Lift each plate from a package opened fully enough to permit this. This prevents scratching a plate by dragging the sharp corner of another plate across it. Working with plates on a clean surface and using thoroughly cleaned tools also helps prevent scratching or otherwise marring a plate.

It is extremely important not to bend or crease an offset plate. Any bend, wrinkle or bulge in a plate will prevent good negative-to-plate contact during exposure. This encourages halation problems. To avoid bending or kinking small plates, carry them by two adjacent corners at the top or bottom of the plate, with the image surface facing away from any machinery, tables or other sharp-cornered equipment. Carry larger plates by two diagonally opposite corners with the image surface of the plate facing up. The largest size offset plates usually require two workers or the use of a mobile hanger for safe and easy handling. Exercise care in handling plates both before and after processing to prevent bends and creases.

An offset plate fully processed and ready for the press deserves some thought for its safekeeping until the press operator schedules it for use on the press. Technicians recommend storing press-ready plates in a free hanging, vertical position. With small plates having punched mounting holes or slots, thread two stiff wires through two of the holes, then suspend the wires between wooden bars secured for the purpose to the sides of an open-topped cabinet. As they become ready for use, slip additional plates onto the wires. Use spring clips secured to wires for plates without mounting holes, or punch holes in the ends of these plates to hang them.

Plates hung with air space between them seldom experience noticeable metal oxidation. In addition, dust and dirt won't cling to them provided the plates are stored dry. To provide further protection and insure against moisture damage, tape a thin sheet of non-absorbent paper to the image side of each plate before placing it in storage. If limited space prohibits vertical hanging of processed plates, store them flat, no more than four or five to a stack, and place protective sheets of paper between them. Whether hanging offset plates or laying them flat, always store them face to face or back to back.

Plates for large offset presses require forming or bending on a bending jig prior to installation on the press. The bending jig creates mounting lips or flanges at the leading and trailing edges of the plate. It is necessary to operate the bending jig correctly and form each plate exactly as specified in the press manual. Otherwise the plate will not fit properly on the cylinder and may crack or tear during operation of the press.

Examine the bending jig frequently to be sure it remains in good mechanical condition and perfectly square alignment. The bending jig must produce bends of the proper angle and depth for the press in use. The bends must lie square on the plate and run parallel to each other. The distance between them determines how smoothly the plate fits on the plate cylinder. Measure this distance and compare it with the mounting segment of the cylinder circumference or with the distance between bends as recommended by the press manufacturer.

Handle all offset plates with care during their installation on the press. Mounting a plate crooked causes extra strain on one side or the other. During the press run, the plate may crack or tear at the stress line. A plate that fits loose also may crack under the flex and strain of impression pressures.

Secure each plate with firm, even tension from one side of the cylinder to the other. Avoid overtightening a plate, to prevent unnecessary strain. Mounting a plate so it precisely conforms to the curvature of the cylinder provides the best insurance against plate cracking.

Summary

Offset plates deserve high standards in their care and handling. Handling unexposed plates without due regard to their light-sensitive nature unnecessarily invites problems in the plateroom and at the press. Rough usage of the thin paper or metal plates risks physical defects of varying degrees of seriousness. Offset plates need protection from light, heat, moisture and dirt. Adequate storage facilities for unexposed as well as processed plates guarantee against accidental damage from these sources of trouble.

Plate processing seems to assume a larger role than plate handling in a study of plate problems only because so many more things can go wrong during platemaking procedures. Each plate must be exposed the right length of time at the correct light intensity. The vacuum frame should create a full vacuum to insure good negative-to-plate contact. Remember that any dust or dirt clinging to the vacuum frame glass will impair the exposure.

Once exposed, a plate should be developed carefully with the correct chemicals applied in the proper sequence and with the use of new or thoroughly cleaned tools. Use only chemicals whose strengths remain unimpaired by age, heat, cold or evaporation. Develop each plate the length of time and in the manner specified by its manufacturer, remembering that either underdeveloping or overdeveloping a plate can lead to printing difficulties.

The water used to rinse off the developed plate also can lead to problems if left on the plate. Many platemakers find it expedient to apply gum arabic with the developed plate lying on several sheets of absorbent paper. The paper aids in removing every trace of moisture from the plate's underside.

Because of the wide variety of offset plates in use today, no single set of rules will insure proper exposure, development and gumming of all of them. The platemaker must become familiar with the plate or plates in use, and follow the manufacturer's instructions to the letter unless experience dictates a change in methods. This alone will insure consistent production of acceptable plates that promote trouble-free offset press operation.

Chapter 11
Offset Printing
Ink Problems

Until those working on the problem perfect inkless printing, offset press operators will continue to experience difficulties directly or indirectly caused by lithographic inks. Most difficulties that involve the ink affect the printing or presswork in one of three ways: ink distribution, ink transfer or ink drying. An understanding of the basic causes of different ink problems enables the operator to organize problem-solving steps so as to effect a cure of the difficulty encountered in the least possible time.

In numerous instances, the operator will find that problem prevention works hand-in-hand with problem solving. Every effort directed toward preventing distribution, transfer and drying problems will prove extremely beneficial.

Ink Distribution

If the ink fails to distribute properly across and around all the rollers in the inking system it cannot form the thin even film necessary for professional quality printing. When ink distributes poorly, certain image areas of the plate may receive excessive amounts of color while immediately adjacent areas receive too little ink. The quality of the work suffers accordingly. In an extreme case, ink may pile up on a part of the plate and fill in non-image areas between halftone dots, or a portion of the plate may become so ink-starved that the image appears gray, washed out, or blinded.

Proper setting of the ink fountain blade is of prime importance in obtaining good ink distribution. If one side of the blade is drawn down too tightly against the fountain roller, that side of the inking system will suffer ink starvation. If the blade makes actual contact with the fountain roller, the roller's surface, scraped free of ink, appears shiny. Obviously, the form inking rollers will not receive enough ink directly forward of this area. Failing to draw down one side of the blade tightly enough will have an opposite effect: excessive amounts of ink passing between the fountain blade and the fountain roller floods the inking rollers with too much color.

The operator can do much toward avoiding either an oversupply or an undersupply of ink by pre-setting the fountain. Pre-setting the ink fountain provides a good example of problem prevention. The ink fountain on an offset press can be pre-set at any time prior to the press run. Many operators use the following method.

Before filling the fountain with a supply of ink, draw down all the fountain blade adjusting screws tight enough so that no daylight shows through the gap between the blade and the fountain roller. It may help to position a trouble light beneath the fountain for this operation. Tighten each screw until the light disappears. Be sure to turn in the center screws first and to work outward toward both ends of the fountain, tightening each screw in turn, to avoid forming a buckle in the blade.

With the entire length of the fountain blade drawn against the fountain roller, back off those screws that lie in a direct line with the image area or areas on the plate. Leave the other screws alone. The amount to back off the screws may vary from press to press; with experimentation you will learn to loosen them the correct amount. Try backing off the screws one-half turn at first.

Fill the fountain with ink. With the ductor roller in contact with the fountain roller, turn the latter over by hand until it picks up a full film of ink. Examine the varying thicknesses of this film carefully. When the adjusting screws have drawn the blade close against the fountain roller, only a thin film of ink should appear on the roller's surface. None of the screws should press the blade so tightly against the roller that no ink appears. When you back off the adjusting screws, the ideal film thickness will vary according to the type of ink used, the paper being printed and the weight or size of the image area on the plate.

A second method for pre-setting an ink fountain involves the use of a thin metal feeler gauge in conjunction with background lighting to determine the proper blade-to-roller gap. Operators who use this method claim a metal feeler gauge provides a greater degree of accuracy. First, turn in the adjusting screws all along the blade. Next, back out those screws directly over the image area on the plate to enlarge the fountain gap. Finally, insert the feeler gauge in the gap and adjust the screws so the blade-to-roller "pinch" just permits you to remove the gauge. Select a feeler gauge having a thickness of .030", .040" or .050", depending upon the ink film thickness you want the fountain roller to carry.

With either method, it will probably be necessary to make small adjustments to individual screws once the press run has begun. Nevertheless, pre-setting the ink fountain will prove a definite aid in promoting good ink distribution.

One frequently encountered ink distribution problem occurs when the ink in the fountain fails to follow the turning fountain roller. Press operators say the ink backs away or hangs back from the roller. Often the ink rolls into a rope-like configuration just out of contact with the roller. As a consequence of this backing away, the fountain roller cannot draw enough ink from the supply. Though initially only one area of the print may show the effect, eventually the entire plate will run dry of ink and all the printing areas will fade.

Depending on the press, the size of the job being printed and the type of ink in use, you can approach the difficulty in one of three ways. If the ink fountain holds a small amount of ink, simply "work" the ink with an ink knife periodically throughout the press run. Working a stiffened lithographic ink tends to revitalize its flowing properties, making it more liquid. Draw the knife back and forth several times through the supply of ink, moving it down the slanted blade toward the fountain roller. On a short or medium-long press run, the operator should have to work the ink down into the ink fountain no more than once or twice.

The ink fountains on many offset presses, especially most larger machines, can be fitted with special ink agitators to keep the ink free-flowing and to prevent its backing away. The electric powered agitator, usually cone-shaped, runs on a track attached to the back of the fountain. It can be set to run the full length of the fountain or only a short distance. Positioned so it dips into the supply of ink, the rotating cone keeps the ink constantly agitated. This automatic method for overcoming an ink's tendency to back away from the fountain roller permits the operator to ignore the fountain for long periods of time during a press run. The device usually proves best for large presses handling exceptionally long runs.

The third method involves altering the ink's physical makeup. The operator may wish to make an ink longer and thus more free-flowing when unexpectedly faced with producing a large number of impressions on a press lacking an automatic ink agitator. To increase an ink's length* or flow, add to it a small amount of varnish having a lower viscosity rating than the varnishes already in the ink. Consult the ink supplier for the proper varnish to use. Add ¼ to 1 ounce of varnish for each pound of ink and mix the varnish thoroughly into the ink. Process a small amount of ink at first and observe how it behaves on the press and dries after printing before adding varnish to a whole batch. (If the ink's viscosity is lowered too far, misting may be induced, where a free-flowing, soupy ink flies from the rapidly turning inking rollers to form a mist of ink molecules in the atmosphere immediately around the press.) To avoid backing away problems in the future, consult the ink supplier, who can furnish an ink having all the desirable properties for the job as well as adequate flow.

Sometimes an old ink will fail to follow the fountain roller or to distribute satisfactorily through the inking system no matter what is done in an attempt to improve its flowing characteristics. If working the ink or adding varnish to it have little or no effect on it, the ink probably has livered. Livering usually results from an irreversible chemical reaction between the coloring pigment and an ingredient in the vehicle. When the viscosity of an ink increases until the ink becomes a stiff, practically unworkable mass, the ink should be discarded or returned to the ink maker for a possible adjustment.

---

*If some ink is placed on a slab and a finger is dipped into it the ink can be drawn out into a thin ribbon or thread. At a certain point the thread will break. The term length evolved from this familiar characteristic of stiff, slow-moving liquids. Long inks can be drawn into relatively long threads. The ribbon of a short ink may break in two before the finger lifts an inch above the slab.

Poor ink distribution throughout the inking system and across the plate frequently coincides with a condition known as water-logging. Water-logging, or water-in-ink emulsion, quickly follows when excessive fountain solution fed to the dampening rollers over-powers a lithographic ink's ability to repel moisture.

As the ink takes on water, it becomes short and buttery. Its internal cohesiveness breaks down and it fails to distribute as it should. The ink may pile or cake on the rollers and on the plate, filling in non-image areas of halftones. As a water-logged ink loses color strength, blacks tend to print gray and color solids appear weak and watery. Individual droplets of water may come between ink and paper to create snowflake-like specks in printed solids and halftone shadow areas.

To reverse the effects of water-logging, decrease the amount of moisture fed to the dampening system. If water-in-ink emulsion has advanced beyond the point of producing a snowflake print, fresh ink may have to be put in the fountain and the press washed. Some inks seem especially prone to water-logging due to an unusually low or unusually high viscosity rating. These inks may benefit from the addition of a varnish of compensating viscosity. Add a heavy or medium-heavy varnish to a soft, soupy ink or mix a light, water-resistant varnish into a short, heavy-bodied ink. Occasionally, an ink fresh from the factory will waterlog because the vehicle has had insufficient time to thoroughly "wet" the pigment particles.* Allowing fresh ink to season for a week or so before use should prevent water-in-ink emulsion from this cause.

Though water-logging can cause an ink to pile or cake on the inking rollers, the plate or the blanket, other factors also can bring about a piling condition. An extremely short ink may pile or cake even though it follows the fountain roller reasonably well. When piling occurs with a short, stiff-bodied ink, add to it a manufacturer-recommended varnish to increase its flow. A poorly

---

The coloring pigment particles in some inks have a marked affinity for water. The thirsty pigment particles attract and hold droplets of water and so envelope themselves with moisture that the supporting medium, the vehicle, cannot keep them under control. If the operator suspects a moisture-loving pigment has caused an ink to waterlog, he should ask the manufacturer to reformulate the ink.

ground ink may contain coarse, heavy pitment particles that cling to and build up or pile on roller, plate and blanket surfaces. The varnishes in the ink cannot keep the overlarge aggregates in suspension and distribute them evenly down through the ink chain. Return a poorly ground ink to the manufacturer for regrinding.

Some heavily pigmented inks, such as chrome yellows, contain an unusually large number of pigment particles per gram of ink, while other inks may contain pigment particles that have a higher specific gravity than that normally encountered. Either excessively heavy or excessively numerous pigment particles may pile or cake if the ink vehicle is unable to keep them in proper suspension during distribution. These inks also might best be returned to the manufacturer for an adjustment or reformulation if serious piling occurs.

Sometimes a piling condition on the blanket surface results when the operator runs too much ink on the first unit or units of a multicolor press. The excess ink on the printed sheet piles or cakes (some say "offsets") on the blankets of succeeding units. Running a lithographic ink in as thin a film as possible consistent with obtaining good reproductions helps prevent this type of piling.

Ink that dries on the rollers obviously will not distribute properly. Ink can and occasionally does dry on the rollers of an offset press while the machine is in operation. The drying ink will pile and cake and build up in a thick, gummy mass on the rollers. As the drying progresses, the underfilm of ink becomes a hard glaze that partially destroys the rollers' affinity for ink and inhibits their ability to distribute it efficiently.

Excessive drier, especially in an ink used on a hot summer day, can cause rapid drying of an ink that at other times performs well. If the fountain solution pH becomes too acid the ink may dry on the rollers while failing to dry on the printed sheet. Changing to a different ink, in the case of excessive drier, or renewing the fountain solution should end the difficulty.

An annoying side-effect often accompanies rapid drying of an ink on the press rollers. As the dried ink builds up on the rollers, tiny, hard particles of the dry ink crust break loose and work down through the chain of rollers to the plate. Here, they cling tenaciously to the plate and prevent full contact with the plate surface by the form inking rollers. As a result, tiny, doughnut-shaped white areas surrounding small points of ink appear in the printed image. We call these nuisances dried-ink hickies. Their removal often entails stopping the press to wash the plate.

Dried-ink hickies and non-distributing ink that has dried on the press rollers illustrate the close relationship between many of the operating difficulties that arise in offset printing. In preventing or overcoming one difficulty, often one or several other closely related problems are solved.

Ink Transfer

The evenly distributed film of ink also must transfer properly from surface to surface during the printing process to insure acceptable reproductions. If the plate, the blanket or the paper surfaces acquire too much or too little ink in the image areas, or if the ink covers these areas unevenly, the quality of the work will diminish.

A serious printing problem arises when ink transfers from the rollers to the non-image areas of the plate. This faulty type of ink transfer we call scumming. Scumming shows up in the printed material as undesirable smudging or dirtiness. Scumming indicates that the affected non-image areas of the plate's surface have become sensitized enough to attract molecules of ink from the form rollers. The problem may affect small, widely scattered areas of the plate, or it may occur in narrow bands across or lengthwise of the plate. Scumming also may occur in the microscopic non-image areas between halftone dots. Assuming faulty platemaking procedures have not produced a plate particularly subject to scumming* the operator may find the ink itself has brought about a condition that has upset the proper transfer of the film of ink.

Offset plate scumming perhaps offers more possible contributory causes to consider than any other single lithographic printing problem. An attempt has been made to associate the condition with each factor that can give rise to it— platemaking procedures, ink formulas, roller surfaces, roller pressures, etc.—to make for easier understanding and quicker recognition of the problem. An awareness of the possible cause or causes of a difficulty helps the operator decide upon proper corrective measures to take.

The ink being run can cause plate scumming in several ways. An abrasive ink that contains overlarge or improperly ground coloring pigment particles may lead to scumming simply by wearing away some of the protective gum coating in the non-image areas. These areas of the plate quickly become ink receptive, and unpatterned smudges appear in the print. The condition tends to worsen as the press run continues and larger non-image areas of the plate become sensitized. Running normally pigmented ink in an excessively thick film can have the same effect. The form rollers mash a heavy film of ink onto the plate. This may overcome the resistance of both the gum coating and the protective film of fountain solution covering the plate's non-image areas. An extremely soft or soupy ink also will lead to scumming if the ink fills in the non-image areas between halftone dots. If this persists, these areas become sensitized and the condition worsens to spread throughout the halftone. Too much drier in the ink also can cause plates to scum under certain conditions.

To prevent ink-caused plate scumming, you likely will have to change to another ink in the case of large or poorly ground pigment particles. Otherwise, running the ink as stiff and as spare as possible consistent with good printing should help prevent scumming. If scumming occurs in conjunction with a very soft ink, add a high-viscosity varnish to the ink. When paper or pressroom conditions call for the addition of more than one ounce of drier per pound of ink, use a concentrated drier to prevent the development of plate scum from this source.

The majority of ink transfer problems occurs when the ink transfers from the blanket surface to the surface of the material being printed. Ink that covers the plate's image areas in a clean, sharp, non-smudged film of the correct thickness, and similarly adheres to the rubber blanket surface, may fail to transfer properly to the paper or other material. Some of the ink may refuse to leave the blanket surface at all, but instead may pull or tear bits of paper fiber or surface coating material from the running sheets. These paper particles distribute through the inking system with predictable consequences, and black specks (hickies) appear in the printed image to mar the finished work.

Paper picking almost invariably is a direct result of an ink having excessive stickiness or tack. Tack relates to the force required to separate an amount or film of ink into two smaller portions or thinner films. An extremely tacky ink strongly resists forced separation. When the surface of the material being printed proves unequal to the task of pulling ink from the blanket, that is, "trapping" the ink, a reverse trapping or capturing of paper particles by the ink occurs.

The tack of a lithographic ink can be decreased by adding to it a varnish having a lower viscosity rating than the varnishes making up the ink's vehicle. Try adding a small amount of No. 00 varnish to a tacky ink. Mix the varnish well into the ink. Before attempting to reduce an ink's viscosity, and tack, it is a good idea to check with the ink supplier or otherwise ascertain that this will not impair other attributes of the ink such as covering capacity and color strength.

Remember, too, that in multicolor presswork, the first-down inks need more tack than succeeding colors to insure a correct sequence of trapping by one ink of the next color printed. A first-down ink lacking sufficient tack may lift from the printed surface under the stronger pull of the next color or colors during later printings. This will result in a splotchy or mottled print and a poor translation of color tones in the finished product. Ink makers usually formulate multicolor or process inks with a definite printing sequence in mind so that each color has somewhat less tack than the ink it will overlay on the printed sheet. Either altering the printing sequence of multicolor inks or changing the tack of one of the colors likely will bring about trapping problems and result in unsatisfactory reproductions.

Mottle, another ink transfer problem, appears most pronounced as a spotty, uneven print in solids and deep shadow areas of halftones. Ink mottle frequently coincides with the use of an ink extremely low in tack. Lacking sufficient tack, the ink fails to transfer evenly onto the printed surface. The operator can increase an ink's tack by adding to it a high-viscosity varnish or body gum. Increasing the pigment/vehicle ratio also gives an ink more tack. If pigment is added to an ink its color strength is increased as well as its tack and this permits running the ink in a thinner film, further amplifying its effective tackiness and preventing mottle.

Sometimes a secondary mottle occurs in conjunction with an ink containing a thin, penetrating varnish. If the varnish penetrates deeply into the printed sheet it affects the transfer of ink onto the reverse side of the paper during a second printing. The penetrated varnish eventually may dry enough to permit printing. Otherwise the first side will have to be reprinted with a different ink, one with less penetrating varnishes and oils.

Running excessive moisture to the dampening system also can result in ink mottle. As water enters the film of ink on the inking rollers, the ink becomes short and pasty, and its tack, its internal cohesiveness, deteriorates. To avoid mottle from this cause, keep the dampening water at an absolute minimum.

With some inks, satisfactory setting and drying of the printed ink film depends on deep penetration of the printing surface by the varnishes and oils that make up the ink vehicle. Such an ink usually contains a higher ratio than normal of low-viscosity, non-drying oils.

A difficulty can arise, however, if an extremely free-flowing varnish enters the paper fibers lying immediately outside the area of the imprint and draws some of the coloring pigment with it. This bleeding of ink into areas closely surrounding the printed image imparts a fuzzy appearance to the print. On many surfaces, production of sharp, clear images requires the use of inks that do not run or bleed into non-image areas of the sheet but do penetrate far enough into the paper to insure proper drying and binding of the ink to the surface. Before printing on a porous or markedly fibrous paper surface, it pays to submit a sample of the paper to your ink supplier, who can then furnish inks suited to the material.

Ink Drying

Failure of an ink to dry on the printed surface can result from one or more of several factors or causes. If the ink contains too little drier it will dry slowly on most printing surfaces and perhaps not at all on some surfaces. Usually, drying problems due to insufficient drier will not arise with a familiar ink, one the operator has used previously and had occasion to test.

To avoid drying difficulties with an unfamiliar ink, whenever possible test it on different surfaces prior to using it in a job of printing. With a clean ink knife, pull thin drawdowns of the ink on a wide selection of paper stocks. Place these samples in a drying rack and test them periodically throughout the day to determine the ink's rate of drying on each surface. With normal inks, the drying rate probably will not vary to any great extent from one surface to another, though the drying rates for different colors of the same type of ink may vary considerably. The operator should be able to handle freely any of the drawdown samples within four to eight hours without smearing the ink. For most commercial purposes, an ink should dry completely within eight hours.

To further assess an ink's drying characteristics, pull another set of thin drawdowns over a few of the drawdown ink films of the first set that have dried. An ink often dries differently when printed over a previously printed film of ink than it does on an uncovered surface. A knowledge of the difference will prove valuable for use with the ink in multicolor printing.

To learn something of an ink's drying characteristics under normal pressroom conditions, sandwich several drawdown samples between sheets of paper. Add weight to simulate sheets stacked on the delivery table of the press. In this way it can be determined how the ink will dry when it has a limited supply of oxygen available to it. Placing the drawdown samples between the pages of a heavy telephone book is another way to make this test.

Any study of an ink's drying properties must take into consideration the ink's principal method of drying. Conventional lithographic inks contain drying oils and driers, and dry by a combination of absorption into the printed surface and by oxidation. These inks work best on uncoated papers. Quick-set inks, designed for use on coated surfaces, contain additional driers, resins and solvents that significantly decrease setting and drying times. Special solvents added to heat-set inks, developed primarily for web-offset presses, evaporate from the printed ink film in the presence of heat. Heat-set inks normally have little practical application on small sheet-fed offset presses.

As even a cursory study of any ink will show, normal drying follows when the ink is printed in normal thicknesses, on normal printing surfaces and under normal press and environmental conditions. To ignore any of these factors invites drying difficulties.

For instance, if the operator runs an ink in an abnormally thick film, say in an attempt to increase the tone or color strength of the print, the ink may refuse to dry, or take too long to dry satisfactorily in time for the promised delivery. Overprinting a heavy, wet film of ink with a drying varnish often proves wasted effort. To add drier to an ink in anticipation of slow drying of a thick film may not solve the problem either. If you print a fast drying ink in a heavy film, the top layer of the ink may dry rapidly to a hard shell that prevents oxygen from reaching the ink below. The dried underlayers of the print may never dry. When using a quick-set ink or an ink to which you have added drier, print in medium or thin films to avoid subsurface drying problems.

A conventional or quick-set ink may fail to dry quickly enough even when printed in a medium or thin film because of other factors. If this occurs, you can run the printed sheets through the press again, overprinting them with a drying varnish, provided the ink has set enough to permit careful handling of the sheets. Apply the drying varnish the same as ink, being sure to remove it from the fountain and inking rollers immediately after use. The ink supplier can provide an overprint or drying varnish suitable for this purpose.

Some operators approach the slow- or non-drying ink problem another way. With the anti-setoff spray device filled with a cobalt solution, the printed sheets are run through the press with the inking and dampening rollers disengaged and the impression off. The cobalt solution, sprayed onto the sheets as they drop into the delivery, brings about a quick and complete drying of the print. A solution of one part cobalt octoate to ten parts naphtha works reasonably well as a drying spray. For plant safety, the naphtha used should have a flash point of 100° F. or higher. You may prefer to consult with your supplier of inks and lithographic chemicals concerning the availability of a suitable commercial spray drier.

Saving a job that failed to dry properly invariably proves much more expensive and time-consuming than the efforts taken to prevent the problem. Thus, the operator always should bear in mind the conditions that may lead to drying difficulties so that these conditions can be eliminated or circumvented.

One cause of poor drying in offset printing, excessive acid in the fountain solution, the operator avoids by maintaining a desirable pH level. A low pH value indicates a high acid content in the fountain solution and should warn of possible drying difficulties. In the presence of acid, cobalt drier changes to an insoluble and inactive chemical compound. Acid renders cobalt drier permanently inactive. As the acidity of the fountain solution increases, larger amounts of the drier in the ink become destroyed. To prevent inhibition or destruction of cobalt drier by acid, keep the fountain solution pH level above 4.0, preferably about 4.5.

The lithographic fountain can also cause drying problems by charging the printed sheets with excessive moisture. Moisture invariably retards drying. Besides the press fountain, the pressroom atmosphere or the paper being printed can provide enough moisture to cause drying difficulties. Moisture from all sources may combine to form a humid environment on and between sheets in the delivery. The effect of moisture on ink drying should not prove permanent; fanning or winding the sheets or blowing hot, dry air through hung sheets should overcome the inhibitory effect of moisture.

Running minimum amounts of moisture to the plate obviously will help prevent serious drying problems from arising. Subjecting relatively moist sheets to the drying effect of a heater or heat lamp at the delivery end of the press will promote ink drying. In humid weather, when the atmosphere becomes heavily charged with moisture, adding more than normal amounts of drier to the ink will decrease drying time of the print. Many technicians recommend adding "drying stimulator" to the fountain solution to promote drying in the presence of excess moisture, which often encourages acid activity. Drying stimulator, available from several ink manufacturers, tends to lower the solution's acid level; at the same time it affects as a drying agent only the ink it contacts on the rollers.

Unless pressroom temperatures can be maintained at 75° to 80° F., drying difficulties may be experienced during the cooler months of the year. A cold atmosphere or a cold printing surface can increase drying time. To circumvent either or both, install an infra-red lamp over the conveyor table to warm the feeding sheets or install a lamp over the delivery pile to warm each delivered sheet.

The operator's normal reaction to drying problems is to add more drier to the ink. This promotes drying unless excessive amounts of drier bring about a reverse action due to the increased amount of non-drying oils added to the ink along with the drier. As in so many other areas of offset printing, while attempting to eliminate one difficulty, secondary or related problems may develop.

For instance if the operator fails to mix the drier thoroughly into the ink, a form of ink mottle may occur. This happens because the poorly mixed drier causes some areas of the printed image to dry at a faster rate than other areas. Some of the print appears dull and part of it appears shiny. Taking time to mix the drier thoroughly into the ink prevents this unnecessary type of mottle.

Most lithographic inks perform satisfactorily most of the time. Nevertheless, due to the large variety of inks available and the increasingly varied surfaces upon which we must print them, the offset press operator must expect occasionally to experience serious distribution, transfer and drying problems. These problems may arise because of an ingredient in the ink, because of the paper being printed, because of pressroom or environmental factors, or a difficulty may originate in presswork procedures. Learning to anticipate, prevent or overcome these difficulties will prove a never-ending but entirely satisfying task to the operator who wishes to achieve and maintain professional status in his chosen trade.

Chapter 12
Fountain Solution
Problems

In offset lithography, the prepared chemical mixture known as the fountain etch or fountain solution has three closely related or complementary functions. First and most importantly, it coats the non-image areas of the plate with a thin film of moisture that prevents ink from adhering to the plate in these areas. In addition, this liquid mixture, largely water, continually bathes the entire plate to keep its surface clean and free of unwanted foreign particles.

The third function of the fountain solution is chemical in nature. Except where dampening systems carry alkaline-based* fountain solutions, the solution mixture will contain a small amount of gum arabic. During the press run, this vital ingredient replaces molecule-for-molecule any of the protective coating of gum that wears away or otherwise leaves the non-image areas of the plate surface.

The gum arabic itself, of course, serves two functions. When spread in a thin coat over the plate during platemaking processes, gum arabic helps protect the plate surface from the effects of oxidation while the plate remains in storage or in transit between the platemaking department and the pressroom. During the press run,

---

*Alkaline-based fountain solutions, on the market since about 1970, contain alakalies and alkaline salts rather than acids and acidic salts. Prepared without gum arabic, alkaline fountain solutions presumably make unnecessary any gumming of the plate during the press run. These fountain solutions tend to have a neutral or alkaline pH value, unlike the more familiar solutions that are acidic in nature.

gum arabic protects the plate surface in all the non-image areas from the sensitizing action of the ink, the inking and dampening rollers and of various chemicals in the ink, the fountain solution and the paper being printed. The gum arabic molecules clinging to the plate surface, being especially water-loving, also encourage retention of a film of moisture by the plate's non-image areas.

Proprietary fountain solution concentrates often have gum arabic as a basic component. In order to have more control over the fountain solution's "gum strength," however, many operators prefer a concentrate that does not contain this ingredient. He may wish to follow this practice. If so, depending upon the type of ink in use, the normal pH level of the fountain solution, the average length of press runs and other factors, mix from ½ to 1 ounce of gum arabic* into 1 gallon of prepared solution. Under no circumstances should more than 1 ounce of gum arabic be added to each gallon of fountain solution. To do so encourages plate blinding or gum streaks on the plate.

Fountain Solution Additives

Fountain solutions also contain small quantities of ingredients such as ammonium bichromate, phosphoric acid and magnesium nitrate. The manufacturer may include these in the original concentrate formula in the proper percentages, or the press operator may prefer to keep a supply of one or more of these chemicals or salts on hand as a fountain solution additive. Each has its special function to fulfill. The exact amount of an ingredient used in a concentrate formula may vary considerably, depending on the plate in use, the kind of papers generally run and other factors that affect the fountain solution.

---

*Technicians generally recommend the use of gum arabic having a Baumé reading between 12° B. and 14° B. Baumé refers to the calibrated scale found on the hydrometer, an instrument chemists use to determine the density values of different liquids. The offset press operator who prepares his or her own gum arabic from basic stock needs a good hydrometer in order to maintain density uniformity from batch to batch.

Some paper surface coatings, for instance, may be alkaline while uncoated papers tend to be acidic. Microscopic particles of paper coating or paper fibers that work back through the chain of dampening rollers eventually accumulate in the supply of fountain solution. As their volume increases, the solution's pH rises or falls accordingly. If the solution becomes excessively acid or excessively alkaline, one of several printing problems may quickly develop. To overcome or prevent the difficulty, slightly increase or decrease the acid content of the fountain solution or the concentrate.

Magnesium nitrate, when added to the fountain solution, insures that pits and scratches or other small breaks in the surface coating on the plate remain desensitized throughout the press run. Many commercially prepared fountain solutions contain magnesium nitrate; most suppliers also offer the desensitizing agent as a separate additive. If a severe scratch problem arises at infrequent intervals or if the concentrate formula in use does not contain magnesium nitrate, a supply may be mixed from which to add small amounts to the prepared fountain solution as needed. A satisfactory formula used in many offset pressrooms calls for mixing 2 pounds of magnesium nitrate into one gallon of water. Add 2 ounces of this mixture for each ounce of fountain solution concentrate used in preparing the final mix.

Other fountain solution additives available to lithographers have special properties designed to combat specific offset printing problems. Mildew and other forms of fungi, for instance, often plague offset printers who live in humid areas. The combination of warm temperatures and standing water encourages fungus, which may grow on the dampening rollers, in the water pan or in the fountain solution bottle. Mildew, if left unchecked, causes cloth dampener roller covers to rot or disintegrate. Fungus in the fountain solution may bring about a change in the solution's pH severe enough to have an adverse effect on the printing. Adding a small amount of a good proprietary fungicide to the fountain solution should prevent the problem of fungus growth.

Under certain conditions of high humidity or if the paper being printed has an unusually high moisture content, the operator may add drying stimulator to the fountain solution to promote rapid drying of the printed ink film. Drying stimulators, available through many lithographic supply houses, do not replace the driers in inks but work with them to hasten drying. As a fountain solution additive, this drying agent affects only the ink that comes in direct contact with the film of dampening water on the plate.

Follow the manufacturer's recommendations to determine the correct amount of drying stimulator to mix into the fountain solution. The amount will range from 2 to 4 ounces of stimulator for each gallon of prepared fountain solution. Used properly, fountain solution drying stimulators prove a valuable aid in preventing drying problems brought on by excessive moisture.

Excess moisture from the dampening system can also cause problems. The nature of the offset printing process requires the use of considerable water. But if we permit more moisture to flow across the dampening rollers than that necessary for good reproductions, one or more of several serious printing problems may occur. Problems such as paper curling, ghosting, faded images, and ink piling as well as slow drying can be caused or aggravated by too much moisture.

Some fountain solution formulas or related factors make it difficult or impossible to reduce the amount of moisture enough to combat the problem or problems caused by excess water without initiating other difficulties. Under these circumstances, we may add alcohol, or one of the available alcohol substitutes, to the fountain solution.

Adding alcohol to the fountain solution permits you to run substantially less moisture through the dampening system. Alcohol reduces the surface tension of water. It makes water wetter. This "wetter" water distributes better through the dampening system and covers the surface of the plate with greater efficiency. Because alcohol evaporates quicker than water, this amount of the total fountain solution liquid does not remain for long in the paper or the ink or anywhere else in the press where moisture might present a problem.

Generally, a fountain solution mixture containing from 10 to 25 percent alcohol works best. Since conditions vary from one printing plant to another, this requires some experimentation.

Begin with a 20-percent mixture. Combine two parts alcohol with eight parts of previously mixed fountain solution. For the next job on the press, cut back on the percentage of alcohol in an attempt to approach a ten-percent mixture. Use no more alcohol than the minimum amount needed. To do so wastes alcohol and adds to the printing costs. And, as the percentage of alcohol passes 30, the chance of an adverse effect on the gum arabic in the fountain solution increases.

(In this respect, when using alcohol, always add the gum arabic to the prepared solution. Never combine gum arabic directly with alcohol. In solutions above a 30-percent alcohol concentration or in the presence of pure alcohol, gum arabic coagulates into a gummy mass that refuses to dissolve.)

The alcohol to use is isopropyl alcohol, the kind commonly referred to as rubbing alcohol. Other alcohols are either too expensive (ethyl alcohol), highly toxic (methyl or wood alcohol), or permeate the atmosphere with unpleasant odors (butyl alcohol). Isopropyl alcohol evaporates rapidly and doesn't harm the skin.

Because alcohol evaporates rapidly when exposed to the air, often more of it must be added to the fountain solution during long press runs in order to maintain the desired alcohol-to-fountain solution ratio. Unless an alcohol tester* is available, determining how much more alcohol to add may prove difficult. On smaller presses lacking an alcohol metering device, many operators mix up a batch of solution and alcohol, fill the fountain solution bottle and place the bottle on the press. When enough solution has drained from the bottle to fill the water fountain, the liquid in the bottle is replenished with alcohol only. As this stronger mix flows into the fountain, the extra alcohol compensates for any loss of the chemical due to evaporation.

The use of alcohol in lithographic fountain solutions may have one serious drawback. Because of its relatively low flashpoint, the

---

Some lithographic supply houses now offer simple alcohol testers that work on the order of battery testers used in service stations and garages. An amount of fountain solution drawn into a glass tube causes one or more balls inside the tube to rise and float near the liquid's surface. The operator determines the percentage of alcohol present in the fountain solution by counting the number of balls afloat.

lowest temperature at which the gases of a combustible liquid will ignite, alcohol can present a fire hazard if not handled properly. Local fire and safety ordinances may require the use of a less volatile substance, such as one of the commercial alcohol substitutes. These products usually have a flashpoint of 100° F. or higher.

Alcohol substitutes work just as alcohol in reducing the amount of moisture needed in dampening systems. Purchased in bulk amounts, they cost no more than alcohol. If you wish to try an alcohol substitute, get one formulated to work in the dampening systems in use. Be sure the substitute will not create other printing problems while solving the problem of excess moisture. Most importantly, purchase an alcohol substitute that meets the anti-pollution and safety standards of the Occupational Safety and Health Act of 1970.

The pH Factor

Besides the problem of measuring or otherwise accurately controlling the amount of alcohol in the fountain solution, the use of the chemical unfortunately presents the operator with another difficulty. Although alcohol has little or no effect on the solution's acid content, it often does render ineffective any litmus pH testing paper immersed in the fountain solution. The alcohol-discolored paper may indicate a pH imbalance that does not exist. This also may be true of some alcohol substitutes. For this reason, technicians advise checking the fountain solution's pH before adding alcohol to it. Alternatively, the operator may use an electric pH meter*, a

---

*Most offset press operators use one of two types of pH testing devices, activated testing papers or an electric pH meter. Activated litmus papers change color when placed in an acid solution. The graduated papers change color only in the presence of certain percentages of acid. The electric pH meter reads the acid level of a solution electronically: an electrode causes a dial on the meter to swing across a numbered scale when the electrode makes contact with the solution being tested. A third method for testing the fountain solution pH involves the use of colored coal tar dyes; a liquid impregnated with a chosen dye will change color slightly according to the liquid's acid content. Full instructions for its use accompanies the testing kit procured.

device that assesses the fountain solution's true acid level whether or not the solution contains alcohol.

The importance of periodically checking the fountain solution pH cannot be overemphasized. On a long press run the solution's acid level often fluctuates markedly. Depending upon the ink in use, the paper being run and other factors, it may increase or it may decrease. Several printing problems can arise or worsen because of an imbalance of the solution's acid level. By maintaining a close watch on the pH factor, the operator can anticipate and prevent these problems by making an occasional adjustment to the acid level.

Normally, you can increase the solution's acid level simply by adding to it a small amount of the fountain solution concentrate. In many cases, the addition of a fraction of an ounce of concentrate returns the solution to a normal pH level. Increasing the percentage of water in the solution will decrease its acid level. In the case of critical presswork and where contamination from the paper or the pressroom atmosphere has dirtied the solution, the best course usually will be to mix up a fresh batch of fountain solution having the desired pH reading.

The correct acid level of the fountain solution may vary slightly depending upon the type of plate in use. Manufacturers of different plates recommend specific pH levels for clean printing and quick drying. Strive to follow these recommendations at all times. The normal range will lie between 3.8 and 5.5 or 6.0 on the pH scale—a scale reading from 0, acid, through 7, neutral, to 14, alkaline. A test of fresh fountain solution should indicate a pH only one or two degrees higher or lower than the level recommended by the plate manufacturer. In testing the fountain solution pH, never round off the result to the nearest whole number. Include the decimal point in your calculations. Remember that a solution testing at 3.8 pH will have an acid level ten times higher than a solution testing at 4.8 on the pH scale.

The problems associated with an imbalance of fountain solution acidity include scumming, plate blinding, roller stripping and poor drying of the printed ink film.

Excess acid in the fountain solution has an adverse effect on the drier in the ink. Any time the pH level drifts to or below 3.8, on the acid side of the pH scale, the operator should restore the solution to its normal acid concentration. If drying problems persist, the solution's acid level may have to be decreased more than the amount specified by the plate manufacturer. For most plates, a pH level between 4.5 and 5.5 will help prevent drying problems.

Plate scumming can result from too much or too little acid in the fountain solution. Usually excess acid will prove to be the cause. On long press runs the acid has time to attack the protective coating on the plate's non-image areas. This promotes scumming. If the acid level decreases markedly during the press run, a light scum in the form of an overall tint may occur. This happens because insufficient acid impairs the ability of the gum arabic to adhere to all non-image areas of the plate. To avoid scum, always maintain a correct pH level in the fountain solution.

Plate blinding often follows a plate scumming condition that involves heavy ink piling. As the ink piles across the image areas of the plate, these areas become worn. This permanently damages the plate, which will remain blinded even though the scumming situation clears up with adjustment of the fountain solution's acid level.

Roller stripping, where the ink fails to adhere to the inking rollers in narrow bands around their circumferences, often indicates a condition of excess acidity. Roller stripping can arise from other factors such as glazed roller surfaces and poor washup practices. However, if the stripping develops suddenly, after several thousand impressions of a long press run, check the fountain solution pH and make any changes needed.

Tinting

Tinting, as the term suggests, appears as a light, uniform film or print of the color being run. The tint covers all the non-image areas of the printed sheet, including the microscopic areas between individual halftone dots as well as the margin areas outside the basic form. At first the operator may believe a scumming situation has developed, and take steps designed to overcome this problem. Before doing so, however, take time to wash the tint from the plate, using plain water at first. In tinting, unlike plate scumming, the film of color on the plate usually will wash away with a wet sponge.

If still uncertain as to whether a tinting or a scumming condition exists, another simple test might be employed. Polish a small square in the non-image area of the cleaned plate with a snakeslip or wet hone. Desensitize the honed area with a sponge dampened with fountain solution, then run sheets through the press until the tint appears again. Examine the last sheets printed to see if the honed area has accepted ink. If it has not, you probably have encountered a plate scumming condition caused by improper platemaking procedures. If the cleaned area on the plate has accepted color, the encountered difficulty probably is tinting.

Tinting occurs when some of the coloring pigment particles bleed into the fountain solution from the ink. This eventually discolors the film of moisture carried by the dampening rollers. So long as the dampening water remains discolored, the printed sheets will carry a tint or shade of the ink. The discoloration or tinting has little to do with the condition of the plate itself, but involves the manner in which the ink reacts to the fountain solution.

The operator knows about water-in-ink emulsion, where moisture penetrates the film of ink carried by the inking rollers and impairs the print. Tinting occurs because of an opposite type of emulsion, ink-in-water emulsion.

Some inks tend to bleed into the fountain solution more readily than others. Many operators test an unfamiliar ink before using it. To test an ink's inclination to bleed, place several drops of fountain solution concentrate on a small amount of the ink you have smeared on a glass or other smooth surface. With a fingertip, attempt to rub the concentrate into the ink. If the ink and concentrate mix readily, this indicates the ink has little resistance to admixture with a liquid and should be replaced or reformulated.

Occasionally, ink-in-water emulsion, and tinting, occurs with a soft ink, one extremely low in viscosity. The varnishes in an ink need a certain level of viscosity in order to hold the pigment particles in suspension. In the presence of water, some of the coloring pigment may escape. If tinting occurs with an ink low in viscosity, stiffen the ink with a more viscous varnish.

Allowing the fountain solution pH level to rise above 6.0 also may result in tinting with some inks. Alkaline paper surface particles gathering in the fountain solution can upset the solution's pH balance. If adjusting the pH by adding to the fountain solution a small amount of solution concentrate does not end the difficulty, try changing to a different paper. Changing to another paper probably will prove necessary if the paper contains a surface active agent that, by lowering the surface tension of the fountain solution too far, encourages dispersal of the coloring pigment particles.

As can be seen, although tinting is considered by most to be a fountain solution problem, the basic cause or causes for this condition usually lies outside the solution itself. For the most part, maintaining the solution's pH level between the outside limits of 3.8 and 5.5 or 6.0 will prevent tinting as well as many other printing problems.

Besides the solution's pH value, you should also take into consideration its temperature when faced with any of the printing problems associated with fountain solutions. If the solution becomes overheated, chemical reactions between different ingredients in the solution tends to speed up. The acids, that in a solution standing at 50° F. have little or no effect on the plate, may in a solution having a temperature above 80° F. rapidly bring about a deterioration of the plate's protective gum coating. Extremely low temperatures on the other hand may cause certain fountain solution ingredients to coagulate. For best printing results, maintain the fountain solution temperature between 50° F. and 80° F.* Try to keep the temperature steady, at least throughout a given press run, to prevent extreme fluctuations of chemical activity.

Distilled Water and Alkaline Fountain Solutions

In mixing up acid based solutions, technicians recommend the use of distilled water where available rather than ordinary tap water. This is because the minerals and possible chemical con-

---

Several lithographic supply houses offer thermometers designed especially for use with water fountains on offset presses. A Centigrade rather than a Fahrenheit thermometer may be preferred.

tamination found in ordinary tap water or spring water often can have an adverse effect on acid based solutions. Many offset press operators use tap water and experience no serious difficulty. But if printing problems such as plate scumming occur or if the plate loses its image after only a few thousand impressions, consider using only distilled water in mixing up the fountain solution. Remember that rainwater contains none of the minerals commonly found in groundwater. Rainwater stored in clean containers can provide an excellent source of water distilled by nature. Using undistilled water from any source can affect the pH. Where distilled water is unavailable, the operator should read the pH value of each fresh batch of fountain solution so he knows exactly what he is working with.

The new alkaline-based fountain solutions apparently do not need mixing with distilled water. Ordinarily, tap water works well because most alkaline-based fountain solution concentrates reduce readily with either hard or soft water. For this reason alone, offset press operators in many areas of the country have turned to an alkaline-based fountain solution, at least as an experiment.

Since the pH value of an alkaline fountain solution may run as high as 10 or 11 on the pH scale, few of the problems associated with excess acidity will occur with these solutions. The use of an alkaline solution when a paper having acid chemicals in its surface coating is being run may help keep the solution's acidity within limits conducive to good printing. Some operators prefer to use alkaline solutions because the acid-base products aggravate a dermatitis condition on sensitive skin.

Two other benefits that may accrue to the user of alkaline solutions include a reduction of the incidence of roller stripping and paper piling or linting problems.

Before purchasing large quantities of an alkaline-based concentrate, however, check with the manufacturer of the plates intended for use. Some plate manufacturers guarantee printing satisfaction only with an acid fountain solution, one having a pH value below 5.5. Satisfactory use of an alkaline-based fountain solution, as with so many other materials used in offset printing, depends upon a proper marriage of the different products used.

Summary

To help insure trouble-free dampening:

— —Purchase concentrates and all fountain solution additives from reliable dealers in lithographic supplies.

— —Store concentrates and additives in a cool, dark area, and note the purchase date on the label of each container.

— —Mix the ingredients together as recommended by the manufacturer, being careful to use the exact amounts of concentrates and additives specified in the instructions.

— —Prepare each batch of fountain solution in clean receptacles, using reasonably fresh concentrate. Dispose of any concentrate or additive obviously deteriorated from the effects of heat, cold, light or aging.

— —In attempting to overcome a fountain solution difficulty, take all relevant factors into consideration: ink formulas, paper-borne chemicals, atmospheric humidity, solution and pressroom temperatures, solution pH, plate condition, etc.

— —Use an additive only if it will improve the quality of the print.

— —Make periodic tests of the fountain solution pH during long press runs and at the beginning of each short run, and correct or renew the solution if necessary.

— —Test all lithographic inks for resistance to bleeding into the fountain solution in use.

— —Make full use of the various instruments and fountain solution testing devices available to check the solution's pH, its temperature, its density, as well as its general condition and the stability of its chemical makeup.

Chapter 13
Paper Problems
in Offset Printing

The printing paper problems encountered by an offset press operator occur at one or more of the three stations a sheet passes through during a printing cycle: the conveyor or feed table, the printing cylinders, and the delivery table. Some papers, due to weight, finish or cut size, may experience difficulties at all three stations on the press. However, most paper problems occur at one point only.

Paper problems range from sheet wrinkling, tearing and mis-register, through snowflaking, surface picking, and tail-end curl to static electricity and the numerous headaches that accompany this problem. The distinctive characteristics of the various paper problems encountered help the knowledgeable operator pinpoint the causative factor or factors and eliminate, or at least moderate, the difficulty.

Conveyor Problems

Wrinkling, tearing or mis-registering of sheets entering or traversing the conveyor tapes can occur with any type of paper normally printed on an offset press. Several factors can give rise to these feeding and register problems.

Sticking Sheets. If two sheets in the feeder unit stick together, one or both of them likely will fail to enter the conveyor tapes properly. If the lifting and forwarding suckers present both sheets to the pullout rollers (draw wheels), the multiple sheet detector should cause them to be deflected from the conveyor table. Often, however, the top sheet, still caught to the lower sheet, will enter the conveyor tapes at an angle and wrinkle or tear. It may pull the second sheet after it into the pullout rollers and cause a particularly bad jam-up of paper.

Most sticking sheet problems develop from one of three causes:

A relatively common cause is a dull or nicked paper cutter blade. Instead of slicing cleanly through a stack of paper, a dull cutter blade chops through and tightly compresses the sheets together at the cutline. The paper appears glued at the cut edge. A badly nicked blade causes sheets to stick together by leaving a ragged line at the cut edge; the nick left in two sheets interlock to impair their proper separation in the feeder unit.

Keeping paper cutter blades sharp and true prevents this cause of paper sticking. When sheets do stick together, feeding problems can be avoided by fanning or winding each batch of paper placed in the feeder unit. Manually working the cut edges breaks apart sticking or interlocked sheets. Turning the sheets end-for-end so any nicks in the cut edge do not face the printing cylinders also will help.

Fanning or winding previously printed sheets helps prevent paper sticking problems that arise when a particularly heavy ink film or droplets of a liquid anti-setoff spray dry and glue some of the printed sheets together. This type of paper sticking can occur either at the edges or in the center areas of printed sheets. It does not occur often in offset printing where the operator runs the ink sparely or in normal thicknesses, nor in conjunction with powder-form anti-setoff sprays. The seriousness or frequency of this type of paper sticking depends partly upon the surface finish of the paper, highly finished coated stocks proving more susceptible.

It is a good practice to examine previously printed sheets to anticipate possible paper sticking difficulties brought on by dried spray, ink or other substances. Lift a small batch of the printed sheets by thumb and forefinger at opposite (not diagonal) corners and work the sheets to create a buckle of air space between them. Now let the sheets hang down from one corner. Any two sheets that stick together will retain the buckle while the rest will straighten out. Remove the sticking sheets, or carefully separate them by working your free hand between them.

A third type of paper sticking occurs with pressure-sensitive labels. Pressure-sensitive stock is manufactured with three layers — a face stock or printing surface, a protective release liner or backing and, between these, a film of pressure-sensitive adhesive. It is the adhesive material that may cause sheets in the stack to cling together at their cut edges. Cutting or trimming operations squeeze some of the adhesive from between the face stock and the removable backing. The adhesive glues the sheets together.

To prevent paper sticking problems with pressure-sensitive materials, work talcum powder, cornstarch or anti-setoff powder into the cut edges. The powder coats and dries the extruded beads of adhesive and keeps them from sticking any of the sheets together.

This need not consume a lot of time. Spread some powder or cornstarch on clean paper and thoroughly jog all edges of the cut stock in the powder. At the same time, work the sheets in your hands to release any sticking sheets.

Paper Curl. Excessively curled paper also may jam up in the pullout rollers, the multiple sheet detector or the conveyor tapes and wrinkle or tear, or they may enter the printing cylinders at an angle and cause a mis-registered print. All printing papers have some curl, the curl appearing most prominent along the two edges that parallel the paper's grain direction. Some papers curl worse than others. The curl in most offset printing papers usually proves negligible.

The condition may become serious, however, if plant or printing circumstances suddenly subject the paper to a damper environment. The operator of an offset press frequently notices an increase in paper curl when the first printing brings about a marked increase in the paper's moisture content.

To prevent serious paper curling, technicians recommend a period of acclimatization for all offset printing papers. Each package or carton of paper should be given ample time to achieve a temperature and relative humidity balance with the pressroom atmosphere. This stabilization should take place well before the time scheduled for printing. The time required for acclimatization varies according to the weight and finish of the paper, to the size of the package or skid, and to the paper's temperature and moisture content as it enters the pressroom. The average time required for a given paper to become acclimatized usually can be obtained from the paper manufacturer.

A further complication may arise if the stock enters the pressroom from an area having a markedly different temperature.

Paper brought into the pressroom from a cold storeroom and suddenly exposed to the pressroom atmosphere will chill the air in its immediate vicinity. This results in an almost instant curling of the paper as moisture condenses from the chilled air onto the exposed sheets.

Correct paper acclimatization follows a simple, two-step procedure. First, move the paper into the pressroom and leave it *in its wrapper* until it has had time to reach the temperature prevalent in the pressroom. Once paper and pressroom temperatures have equalized, you may open the package to permit the sheets to attain a moisture balance with the surrounding air. It may be best to leave paper cut to printing size in its protective wrapper until just prior to press time in order to minimize the effects of any sudden change of moisture level in the sheets.

Pressure-sensitive materials and other papers especially prone to curling may require special handling during acclimatization. It helps to cover a skid of pressure-sensitive label material with a perfectly flat sheet of plywood and weight the plywood with one or two bricks. This keeps the sheets flat while they come into a temperature/moisture balance with the pressroom so the printing surface or face stock and the protective backing, which give up or accept moisture at different rates, will slide horizontally on the film of adhesive separating them. Without the weight to keep them flat, pressure-sensitive labels may curl into unmanageable shapes as they lose or gain moisture.

When a paper insists on curling, you may have to utilize other methods to prevent feeding and printing difficulties. It is feasible to roll out the curl at the leading edge of most papers by hand. Lay a small batch of paper on a flat surface with the curl down and the leading edge toward you. Separate 6 to 24 sheets from the batch and gently roll back the curled edge, applying only enough pressure with your palms to eliminate the curl. The sheets will remain flat enough to feed through the press without hindrance. This is especially helpful when recently printed sheets have absorbed enough moisture from the press to curl them badly.

Running sheets through an offset press with the grain direction paralleling the line of travel offers another method for avoiding problems that develop from paper curl. This places the curled edges at the sides of each sheet rather than at the leading and trailing ends. However, due to the close relationship between grain direction and paper-stretch registering problems, the operator should not utilize this method in multicolor printing or whenever a close register must be maintained.

To mitigate paper-curl problems, remember to load all the stock in the feeder unit either with the curl up or with the curl down. When the press is set up to accept stock with the curl down, sheets entering the conveyor tapes curl up, may wrinkle and tear.

Sheet Separation. Trouble-free presswork requires the top few sheets in the feeder unit to float freely on the air blast so the lifting suckers can separate the topmost sheet from the stack. For the most part, adjusting the amount and direction of air and the rate of pile ascent for the different weights of paper assure complete separation of the top sheet.

Feeding difficulties occasionally arise with papers somewhat heavier or lighter than those normally printed. Special strategies may have to be applied to get cardweight or flimsy sheets to separate and feed properly.

Manufacturers of many presses furnish or offer for purchase special lifting sucker attachments to use with unusually heavy or lightweight papers. Such attachments, like other devices available from manufacturers, easily prove their value when large quantities of odd-weight papers are printed.

A radical repositioning of the air blowers on some presses may also help achieve good separation of the top sheet. So long as a movable air blower does not interfere with the operation of the lifting and forwarding suckers, the pile height regulator or the pullout rollers, it may be moved to wherever the flexible air hose permits. Remember to examine the air blast holes whenever paper separation problems develop; dirt, anti-setoff powder or paper dust not infrequently plug some of the holes and impair the efficiency of this important feeder unit component. Feeding of card weight papers often improves with heavy blasts of air directed deeper into the stack than normal.

Placing small wooden wedges under the stack of paper in the feeder often improves sheet separation. The wedges create a bulge in the stock so the pile height regulator causes the paper to ascend at an abnormal rate. Shifting the wedges about also will present the top sheet to the lifting suckers at a different than normal angle which often helps. Wedging works best with the printing of lightweight papers in preventing sheet separation difficulties.

Timing. In order for sheets to feed through an offset press without twisting, binding or tearing — at any point in their journey from feed table to delivery table — the machine must operate in perfect timing. Feeding and register difficulties caused by an out-of-time press often imitate those generated by sticking sheets, paper curl or faulty sheet separation.

Timing begins with the first machine-controlled movement of the sheet. The pickup suction applied to the top sheet by the lifting suckers should begin when the lifting sucker feet have achieved maximum dwell, that is, reached the bottom of their downward stroke. To check this, switch on the air and suction, but not the main drive motor, then turn the machine over by hand, carefully observing when the lifting sucker vacuum begins to take the top sheet under control. Continue turning the machine over until the sheet enters the pullout rollers or until the forwarding suckers take over.

If sheet control by the lifting suckers begins too soon or too late, or if the lifting suckers release the sheet prematurely, refer to the instruction manual to determine the proper procedure for correcting vacuum timing. Some presses will require the assistance of a factory-trained serviceman. Remember that unless the lifting sucker vacuum functions correctly, feeding and register difficulties will probably be experienced.

To further check the machine's timing, manually feed a sheet down the conveyor belts toward the end of the conveyor table. As the sheet approaches to within 1/4" to 3/8" of the metal headstops, these thin "fingers" should rise into registering position. Examine them for bends or broken tips. With the sheet near or against the headstops, look at the feed rollers that draw the sheet forward from the conveyor table and into the printing cylinders. These should have opened fully to accept the sheet without crumpling its leading edge. Continue to turn the press over by hand until the headstops drop away and the upper feed roller drops into position to pull the sheet forward. Exact synchronization of all components of the press is vital for trouble-free printing.

Through the Printing Cylinders

As the sheet progresses through the printing cylinders other potential printing problems arise. These involve the ink in use, impression pressures, and moisture — and the way these factors affect the paper.

Paper Picking. Small blemishes called hickies sometimes appear in the image area of the printed sheet. Paper hickies have the appearance either of black dots or tiny, fat threads of fibers encircled by un-inked paper surface. Examination of the blanket's rubber surface will reveal minute particles of paper sticking to it. While these tiny mounds accept ink and print, they prevent printing contact of the paper with the blanket in the microscopic areas immediately surrounding them.

Paper picking, a common cause of hickies, occurs when the ink on the blanket pulls particles from the surface being printed. This happens when the tack or pull of the ink overcomes a paper's resistance to forced separation. The incidence of picking decreases as the ink's tack goes down. The operator can prevent the condition by running an ink having less tack, provided the requirements of multicolor printing or other factors do not preclude its use. Printing an ink in a thicker film also tends to decrease its effective tack. Reducing an ink's tack by adding to it a small amount of No. 00 litho varnish and printing the ink in a slightly heavier film often end paper picking problems.

Technicians who have noted that paper picking often occurs during the first few impressions at the beginning of a press run, before the stiff ink on the rollers has "warmed up" or reached good printing consistency, recommend a judicious application of anti-setoff spray to the inking rollers just prior to starting the press to soften the ink.

Paper picking problems occur more frequently with papers that lack manufactured "pick resistance." Under these circumstances, the problem can be resolved without altering the ink but by changing to a different paper, if this will prove acceptable to the customer.

Before undertaking any of these solutions, examine the trimmed edges of the stock in the feeder unit. Loose paper particles that fall from the running sheets onto the blanket often cause hickies. To rid the stock of lint, loose fibers or paper particles left by the cutting operation, wind or fan small batches until nothing flies from around the cut edges. Faced with a particularly stubborn case of cutter dust or paper lint, try running the paper through the press with the water and ink "off" and the impression "on," periodically wiping the accumulation from the blanket.

Snowflaking. The printing problem referred to as snowflaking derives its name from the appearance of a random scattering of pinpoint- to pinhead-size unprinted areas in the image. The image looks mottled or flecked. The condition develops when tiny water droplets come between the printed surface and the film of ink. This occurs either through water-in-ink emulsion or because moisture adhering to non-image areas of the sheet prevent complete coverage of the surface by the ink film.

Water-in-ink emulsion, also called waterlogging, comes about when water from the dampening system invades the ink traveling the inking rollers. In addition to a snowflaky print, the ink has become short and buttery, refuses to distribute across the rollers properly and may pile or cake on the rollers and on the plate. Reducing the amount of water admitted to the dampening system usually prevents water-in-ink emulsion.

Snowflaking that arises from the second cause, moisture on the sheet being printed, usually occurs only in multicolor printing on a multi-unit press or on a common impression offset press. The ink itself may not have suffered moisture penetration. What happens is that water picked up by the paper from the blanket on the first unit does not evaporate or dissipate into the sheet rapidly enough to permit proper acceptance of ink from the second unit's blanket. Because ink laid down in the first printing tends to reject water, wet-paper snowflaking nearly always shows up only in unprinted areas of the sheet, as it enters the second unit.

To determine if you have encountered wet-paper snowflaking, shut off the first printing unit and print the second color only. This keeps the sheet dry until it reaches the second unit, so that snowflaking should not appear in the second color.

Snowflaking may occur more frequently with coated papers than with uncoated papers. The amount of moisture carried by the dampening rollers also will have an effect. Changing to a different paper or cutting back on the moisture may end the problem.

Printing the heavier of two forms first provides another possible solution to the problem. This helps two ways. Larger image areas ease the task of keeping first-unit dampener moisture to a minimum. In addition you have smaller unprinted areas to contend with in the second printing.

A blower device or small fan directing a stream of air onto the sheets as they pass between printing units hastens evaporation of first-unit moisture and helps prevent snowflaking.

If these methods fail to end the condition, print the job one color at a time or run the press at slow speed to give each sheet more time to dry.

Dot Doubling. Widespread dot doubling spoils the appearance of the printed sheets. A look through the magnifier reveals shadowy duplicates of individual halftone dots printing in some of the non-image areas between the regular dots. Dot doubling usually is linked to the condition of the paper being run. The sheets in the feeder often are badly bulged or wavy, with heavily curled or wrinkled edges.

As a bulged or wavy sheet enters the printing cylinders, the bulge rises prematurely against the inked blanket with enough pressure to cause a light transfer of ink just prior to actual printing pressure. The second contact follows immediately after the first false impression. This double contact of the blanket with the paper surface results in the printing of two halftone dots, one lightly inked and one fully inked, in close proximity where only one dot should print.

Providing a means for moisture/temperature conditioning all paper brought into the pressroom, as described under "Paper Curl," provides the best insurance against dot doubling. Wherever possible use fully acclimated papers that do not curl or wrinkle when exposed to pressroom atmospheric conditions.

To prevent problems associated with bulges, curls and wrinkles, most offset presses have some means of keeping the sheets under physical control as they pass through the printing cylinders.

Small, single-color machines* usually will have a hold-down brush positioned so each sheet must pass between the brush and the impression cylinder. The brush irons out any waves or bulges and keeps the sheet flat against the impression cylinder surface. This prevents premature contacting of the blanket by any part of the sheet. Keeping the brushes clean and in good condition and positioning them correctly helps prevent dot doubling.

Impression Curl. Moisture-balanced sheets may enter the printing cylinders relatively flat, yet fall into the delivery in an extremely curled condition. This problem may occur more frequently with some coated papers, the high gloss and smooth surface of coated stock increasing each sheet's tendency to cling to the blanket. Coated papers also require thinner ink films for sharp, clear printing and the higher tack of thin films of ink encourages paper picking, delamination (layer separation), blanket conformability and paper curl. Change to an uncoated paper or slightly decrease the tack of the ink to prevent paper curl that follows when sheets conform to the blanket cylinder's curvature.

Excessive dampening water also can lead to unmanageable paper curl problems in the delivery. The running sheet may absorb enough moisture from the over-wet non-image areas of the blanket to cause an almost immediate curling of its leading and trailing edges. As in many other offset printing problems, running dampener moisture at an absolute minimum consistent with good reproductions helps prevent paper curl.

Occasionally, serious paper curl problems occur because of extremely heavy printing pressures. Excessive impression crushes the fibers in the sheet as it passes between the blanket and impression cylinders. Certain papers prove more susceptible to crushing than others. To prevent paper curl, back off the impression until the image prints light, then gradually increase the printing pressure until you have an acceptable image on the sheet.

---

*Larger, more sophisticated offset presses may have a hold down air bar. The air bar directs a stream of air at the running sheet just prior to its entry into the impression nip between the blanket and the impression cylinder. With these devices the operator must make sure that the air holes are kept clean and that enough air pressure to keep the sheets flat actually reaches the air bar.

Paper Stretch and Misregister. In addition to pre-impression and post-impression curl, the moisture paper absorbs during offset printing processes can also cause the sheets to stretch. The extent of paper stretch depends on the amount of moisture absorbed. A dry paper exposed to a moist atmosphere will experience a greater size change than a paper having a higher relative humidity. Because individual fibers in paper, when wet, may increase up to eight times more in their diameter than in their length, the greatest sheet-size change occurs across the grain rather than in grain direction.

A dimensional change in the paper being printed ordinarily does not create serious problems except in multicolor presswork, or where it is necessary to obtain a close register of a second printing with the first. Then, if the absorbed moisture generates a large enough sheet-size change between the first and second printing, the second-down image will fail to register with the first.

The same paper-handling procedures recommended for combatting paper curl also help prevent paper-stretch problems. A system for acclimatizing or moisture-conditioning paper brought into the pressroom will help prevent both paper curl and paper stretch. Technicians also recommend maintaining the pressroom atmosphere at a relative humidity rating of approximately 40 percent, and allowing the paper to reach this same RH level before printing.

If the moisture content of the paper can be increased under controlled conditions, bringing it to a higher moisture level than that which obtains in the surrounding atmosphere often proves beneficial in multicolor printing or where the sheets must pass through the press again immediately after the first printing. Paper supercharged with moisture prior to printing tends to release moisture equal to the amount it absorbs during printing. This keeps the paper from stretching at all or at least keeps any size change within tolerable limits.

Because paper stretches* across the grain more than in grain direction, the operator often can overcome paper-stretch misreg-

---

Paper shrinks, of course, following a release of moisture from its fibers into a dryer atmosphere.

ister problems at the press, *provided the stock has been cut to feed with its grain direction running at right angles to the direction of sheet movement through the press.*

It is only necessary to remember this basic fact of offset printing: increasing the number of packing sheets under the blanket has the effect of *lengthening* the printed image in the direction of paper movement or around the cylinder, while overpacking the plate cylinder *shortens* the image. Thus, removing sheets of packing from under the blanket and placing them under the plate will shorten or shrink the image. Conversely, underpacking moved from the plate cylinder to the blanket cylinder lengthens the image.

The effect that the amount of packing on the cylinders has on image lengths permits you to combat most paper-stretch register problems that arise. As a sheet gains moisture during the first printing, and stretches, the image printed on it lengthens accordingly. In order to bring about a register of the second print with the first, move packing sheets from the plate cylinder to the blanket cylinder and increase the image length of the second form. This lengthens all segments of the image equally, just as all areas of the paper have stretched.

To circumvent possible register difficulties in multicolor printing, many operators utilize the foregoing method of image-length control to purposely create a cylinder packing imbalance before making the first run on a single color press or on the first unit of a multi-unit machine.

To do this, take a few packing sheets from the blanket cylinder and place them under the plate. This shortens the image. As the sheet absorbs moisture from the press during the first printing, and stretches, it lengthens the artificially shortened image. Often this brings the image back to its original dimensions so that the second image prints in exact register with it, without further packing sheet changes. If not, moving one or more packing sheets from the plate cylinder back to the blanket cylinder will lengthen the second image enough to bring about a register. This procedure of image-length control works especially well when you must print a relatively dry paper and fear printing processes will cause it to experience appreciable stretching.

Blanket Smash-ups. Blanket smash-ups occur when double or triple thicknesses of the paper being run enter the printing cylinders. The mass of paper exerts crushing pressures against the rubber blanket, mashing down the compressible fibers in the blanket's fabric backing. A bad smash-up will completely ruin a blanket; less severe smash-ups, even after extensive repairwork, often leave the operator with an unsatisfactory printing surface from which sporadic image loss problems develop. Blanket smashups are best prevented through proper handling of the cut stock, through correct press makeready procedures and by maintaining printing pressures correct for the paper being printed.

To prevent the forwarding of two or more sheets at once into the press, avoid placing sheets having ragged or knicked edges in the feeder unit. The nicks in two sheets often interlock and cause both sheets to be drawn into the conveyor tapes. Take time to fan or riffle the gripper end of each batch of cut paper you place in the feeder unit. This forces air between the sheets and aids the air blower's task of separating them. Build a straight, even stack of paper to prevent twisting and misfeeding of any of the sheets as they travel down the conveyor belts. Twisted or misfed sheets often result in blanket smash-ups. Remove folded sheets, half sheets and sheets of irregular thicknesses from any batch of makeready paper placed at the top of the stack in the feeder.

Whenever possible, avoid the use of second- or third-rate papers. Use the highest grade of stock the job in progress will warrant. The high incidence of half sheets, spliced sheets, miscut sheets and hidden ream markers in cheaper grades of stock make these papers a prime cause of blanket smash-ups.

Simply adhering to proper makeready procedures does much toward preventing blanket smash-ups. Set the lift of the feeder unit so the top sheet in the stack rises to the distance below the sheet separators prescribed in the instruction manual. Otherwise, the lifting stack may interfere with the sheet separators so the lifting suckers tend to remove more than a single sheet from the top of the stack. In addition, adjust the air blowers to separate only the top three or four sheets, set the pullout rollers to make even contact with the sheet and make sure that the conveyor tapes, the hold-down straps or bars, the jogger, the side guide and the head stops all work together to keep the running sheet straight and flat.

While these precautions help insure against blanket smashups, this unfortunate printing problem will occur from time to time. To minimize the seriousness of a smash-up, avoid excessive pressures between the printing cylinders. Use the minimum amount of impression necessary to obtain a sharp, clear image. This will insure that the pressures of a smash-up are not added to impression pressures already placing excessive squeeze on the blanket. It may help, too, to use relatively soft, compressible packing sheets under the blanket so a percentage of smash-up pressures vents itself against the more expendible underpacking.

In the Delivery

As the printed sheets leave the printing cylinders, trouble may develop if they fail to drop freely from the delivery chain grippers and lie straight and flat on the delivery table. Wrinkling and tearing of the sheets and ink smearing or setoff are the more common difficulties encountered here. Besides delivery table jogger and side guides incorrectly set for the stock being printed, two other factors often lead to delivery problems.

Delivery Chain Grippers. As the printed sheet enters the delivery, it comes under control of the delivery chain grippers. The chain itself must turn in perfect timing with the printing cylinders so transfer of the sheet from the impression cylinder grippers to the delivery chain grippers occurs without mishap. In addition, all the grippers must operate freely, open fully and exert even pressure when clamped on the sheet's leading edge.

Both chain and grippers need periodic cleaning and careful oiling to keep the delivery operation running smoothly. Also, clean and examine the activating pawls that control the opening and closing of the grippers. Any dirt or hard foreign particles can interfere with their movement.

Usually, delivery chain problems occur with only one set of grippers. If each gripper bar is painted with a stripe of different colored paint, this will ease the task of locating the troublesome grippers.

With the chain in time and the grippers operating smoothly, serious delivery chain problems should not occur.

Static Electricity. Static electricity refers to an electrical charge that is basically at rest (static) in the charged material. A material becomes electrostatically charged when some of its atoms become unbalanced in their normal complement of electrons. The affected atoms either will have lost one or more of their orbiting electrons or they will have acquired more electrons than they normally possess.

In offset printing processes, this usually occurs through contact electrification, where the atoms in one material give up electrons to those in another material in physical contact with it. Movement of one material across another increases the effect of contact electrification because this increases the number of contact points for the exchange of electrons.

On an offset press, as a sheet of paper moves rapidly along and in partial contact with a metal conveyor table, the more conductive metal releases electrons into the paper. Then, as the paper moves out of contact with the table, these electrons remain trapped in the sheet, giving it a negative charge. Thereafter, the paper attempts to release the excess electrons into some other material.

The static electricity generated in paper causes printing problems primarily because of the nonconductive* nature of paper. This nonconductivity prevents the ready transfer of electrons so that a sheet, once charged, cannot quickly return to an electrically neutral state. As the excess electrons strive to leave the charged sheet they cause it to cling to whatever material it contacts. This may occur along the conveyor table, in the printing cylinders or in the delivery where printed sheets cling tightly together.

The conductivity of paper changes markedly with its moisture level or relative humidity. Paper loses conductivity, and its ability to resume a neutral state, electrically, as its moisture level decreases. As its fibers take on moisture, a paper's conductivity rises.

Concerning conductivity, copper and silver readily give up or take on electrons and therefore make good conductors. Rubber and glass, the atoms of which hold tightly to their orbiting electrons, make good nonconductive insulators. Paper is neither a nonconductor of electricity (it will not insulate) nor is it a good conductor (electricity will not "flow" through paper as through copper.)

Thus, dry paper retains an electrostatic charge, with resultant feeding, printing and delivery problems, for longer periods than relatively moist papers. In a print shop lacking an efficient air conditioning system or some means of humidity control, static problems abound during periods of low humidity such as wintertime months that see the use of furnaces and heaters. As paper comes into equilibrium with an atmospheric relative humidity of 40% or slightly higher, and the paper's conductivity rises correspondingly, static electricity problems abate.

The best way to prevent static buildup in paper, then, is through air conditioning or humidification of the pressroom. Lacking a means of atmospheric control, the operator must rely on other methods for combating static electricity.

Several printing supply houses offer static eliminators designed to prevent the difficulty. When used according to directions, these devices have proved an invaluable aid in many pressrooms plagued with static.

A less effective method involves draping anti-static tinsel across the press to let the traveling sheet give up its electric charge. The problem here is that the nonconductive paper spends too little time in contact with the tinsel to see the release of much static.

Realizing static electricity proves most bothersome on days of low humidity, and creates more feeding and printing difficulties with some stocks than with others, the operator can often control or moderate static through a simple rescheduling of the jobs being printed. Exchanging a paper that seems especially subject to the effects of static for another paper otherwise equally suitable for the job may prevent problems. Because a static buildup increases quicker when the sheets pass rapidly through the press, running the machine at slower speeds offers another means for static electricity control.

We certainly cannot blame all "paper problems" exclusively onto the paper we use. Press makeready, cutting operations, inks and fountain solutions, as well as changing atmospheric conditions also play a part. Whenever a paper problem arises, take the time necessary to analyze it fully before commencing corrective measures. This saves time and material and increases the effectiveness of your troubleshooting efforts.

Chapter 14
Troubleshooting
Unsuspected Causes of
Offset Press Problems

Occasionally, the operator of an offset press encounters a press or printing problem, the underlying cause of which seems to defy detection. Such problems include feeding and register difficulties, faulty impression pressures, assorted ink-related troubles, dampening problems and difficulties involving basic press maintenance.

The following unusual and frequently unsuspected causes of printing and operating difficulties represent only a small percentage of the numerous specific causes or causitive factors of this nature. Technicians and offset press operators of considerable experience will have faced and overcome these and many other instances of unsuspected problem producers. For the beginning or apprentice operator, however, a study of the material presented here will prove valuable in the search for answers to different printing problems. Hopefully, too, it will encourage offset press operators to look beyond the obvious and more common causes of offset printing problems when initial troubleshooting steps fail to produce the desired results.

Feeding and Register Difficulties
Unlevel Press and Press Vibration. The factory serviceman who installs a press in a printing plant adjusts the press to set level and makes sure the machine rests solidly on its foundation. If the press subsequently is moved from its original location or if the floor becomes uneven through foundation settling, the press no longer will set level. If three "legs" of the press make contact with the floor, but the fourth does not, the machine may develop a tendency to

vibrate during operation. Unless an offset press sets solidly on its foundation as well as perfectly level, side-to-side and front-to-back, several printing problems can occur.

In the lift or feeder unit of an unlevel, vibrating press, the top sheets in the stack tend to drift toward the low end or side of the press. If the feeder unit side guides, the blower and the sheet separators fail to keep the drifting sheets under complete control, they may enter the pullout rollers improperly and jam, wrinkle or tear as they traverse the conveyor tapes. On a machine having a decided tilt to one side or the other, the sheets may enter the conveyor tapes properly but drift to an out-of-register position as they travel along the conveyor table. This can result in sporadic tearing, wrinkling or misregister difficulties as the sheets enter the printing cylinders.

The floor or the building foundation itself, unless absolutely rigid and completely free from vibration, can cause register difficulties by transferring ground tremors to the press. A vibrating floor can greatly magnify ground tremors caused by passing freight trains or huge trucks. Any sudden, violent jar may jiggle closely set registering devices on a press out of adjustment. Shoring up an unstable foundation or moving the press onto a concrete, non-vibrating floor may end seemingly inexplicable register problems.

Problems other than feeding and register difficulties can result from an unlevel press or from press vibration. Poor ink distribution may occur if ink runs toward the low end of a tilted fountain. Unusual or excessive wear of rollers and other heavy moving parts may occur over a long period of use on an unlevel press. For trouble-free presswork, a machine that sets perfectly level and remains free of vibration is needed.

The operator can easily check the levelness of an offset press with a small, inexpensive carpenter's level. If he discovers the press to be setting unlevel, he should locate and adjust its leveling devices or, if necessary call in a factory serviceman to insure an accurate adjustment. Placing a container of water on different sections of a press or observing the liquid in the water fountain will help detect excessive press vibration.

Press Speeds and Power Fluctuations. On some offset presses, in order to obtain a register accurate enough for multicolor printing, the operator must maintain a constant press speed throughout the entire press run. Operating the press at slow speed during the first half of the first printing and at a higher speed during the second half may yield two prints slightly but measurably out of register with each other on some of the sheets. This can happen if a sheet traveling down the conveyor table at one speed rebounds from the head stops, if only a fraction of an inch, while a sheet moving at a slower speed does not bounce. Or press speed variations can so affect the action of the grippers on the impression cylinder that they pick up otherwise perfectly registered sheets in such a way as to cause misregister. The explanation for unexpected register difficulties during the second printing of a two-color job may prove nothing more complex than the operator having run the press at different speeds during the first printing.

Even with the press set to run at a constant speed, register problems may develop if the power for the drive motor fluctuates during operation of the press. Constant press speeds require a source of power that does not experience large fluctuations. If the power to the drive motor varies, the speed of the press will vary accordingly. A serious power fluctuation (and press speed change) may result in a misregister of those sheets printed during the power drop or surge.

A power fluctuation may prove difficult to detect without the help of an electrician to conduct a thorough testing of the pressroom wiring. Only a qualified electrician should perform any rewiring such a test might indicate as necessary.

Incorrect Lubrication. Serious press speed fluctuations also can result from unwise or inappropriate maintenance activities on the part of the operator, most especially incorrect lubrication. Every moving metal part of an offset press requires lubrication, of the type and at the intervals specified by the manufacturer. In general, each gear, cam or shaft on the press will need one of three basic lubricants: grease, a medium-heavy oil or a lightweight oil. Some moving parts require lubrication at the beginning of each shift of work, while other areas need oiling once a week, once a month or at less frequent intervals. Follow the manufacturer's recommendations as to type and frequency of lubrication in order to insure friction-free operation of the press.

Incorrect lubrication of a press can cause speed fluctuations in two ways. First, if insufficient oil or grease reaches a moving part, the continued friction of bare metal against turning bare metal will cause the unlubricated part to resist the thrust of the drive motor. This tends to slow the press. Depending on the size of the poorly lubricated part, the drop in press speed may or may not prove noticeable or cause misregister. The drag of several insufficiently lubricated parts definitely will cause a slowing of the machine. If a lubrication-starved part runs dry over a prolonged period, the resulting friction may build up enough heat to "freeze" the part and cause serious damage while dragging the press to a complete stop.

Press speed fluctuations also can result from inappropriate lubrication of moving parts. If the operator applies a heavy grease to shafts that work best when lubricated with a light machine oil, the grease may be stiff and unyielding on cool mornings. This will slow the press. Later, when the turning shafts have warmed the grease, the press may operate significantly faster.

Guided by the maintenance manual supplied by the manufacturer, follow a system of lubrication that will keep all moving parts of the press properly oiled and greased. If operating difficulties develop from incorrect or inadequate lubrication, it will pay to thoroughly clean away all the old oil and grease with a good cleaning solvent. This will rid oil holes and grease cups of any accumulated dirt and lint which also can impair lubrication. With all parts clean, apply fresh lubrication to the press.

Printing Cylinder Difficulties

Unsatisfactory Images, Press Wear and Faulty Impression Pressures. Correct impression or printing pressures, between the plate and blanket cylinders and between the blanket and impression cylinders, will prove of utmost importance to the operator of an offset press. Without correct impression pressures, satisfactory printing will elude the operator. Different weights or grades of paper and different kinds of ink require different impression pressure. Ideally, the amount of printing pressure will be that which produces sharp, clear images, and no more.

Assuming the operator has followed the instruction manual for the press to correctly set the cylinder pressures for the ink and paper being used, excessively heavy or excessively light impression pressures still may result from incorrect plate or blanket cylinder packing. The importance of using the amount of underpacking recommended by the press manufacturer cannot be overemphasized. In addition to the immediate problem of unsatisfactory reproduction, either too much or too little packing eventually will result in an excessive wearing of the cylinder bearers and cylinder teeth and other parts of the press. Continued wearing of the cylinder bearers may create an out-of-roundness that will prevent you from ever achieving a good print.

Even underpacking sheets in carefully calculated thicknesses may indirectly cause faulty impression pressures if the sheets absorb enough moisture during plate or blanket washups to swell appreciably. This may yield a light print, if the packing sheets swell enough at the outer edges to hold the center portions of the blanket from good printing contact with the plate.

More probably, packing sheet swelling at the edges will result in mourning-band scum, a condition where the outside edges of a plate become ink-receptive. As moisture from the dampening system seeps in under the plate during operation of the press or as solvents wick under the plate or blanket during washups, the edges of the packing sheets often swell enough to increase to a substantial degree the plate-to-blanket pressure in these areas. This pressure gradually wears away the desensitizing film that protects the non-image areas, in bands running lengthwise of the plate. These worn areas eventually become highly ink-receptive. The result is undesirable bands of ink (scum) in the print.

Avoiding the use of excessive amounts of liquid washup solutions and cutting the packing sheets fractionally narrower than the plate or blanket helps prevent moisture from wicking into the layers of underpacking. A very light film of oil applied to the cylinder surface near the outer edges of packing sheets will form a moisture barrier to keep washup solvents and fountain solutions from affecting the sheets.

Creeping Packing Sheets. A film of oil applied to plate and blanket cylinder surfaces also may help prevent another printing problem, that of creeping packing sheets. During a press run, the stress of plate-to-blanket impression pressures may cause one or more sheets of packing to creep. Such creeping usually occurs in conjunction with heavy printing pressures.

If the packing sheets creep far enough, the print obviously will suffer. First, a light band in the print appears near the leading edge. As the packing sheets continue to creep, the light area enlarges in size, ruining the printed sheets.

If possible, cut the packing sheets long enough to provide ¼ " to ½ " to tuck into the forward clamping device along with the plate or blanket. If circumstances do not permit this, use small dabs of glue around their edges to band all the packing sheets together, then secure the sheaf of packing sheets to the blanket or plate with a strip of masking tape. Clamp the completed assemblage of plate (or blanket) and packing sheets to the cylinder in the usual manner, being careful to smooth out any wrinkles in the sheets of underpacking.

A single sheet of underpacking can usually be kept in place if the operator smears a film of oil or medium weight grease on the cylinder surface and presses the packing sheet onto this as you install the plate or blanket.

Slippage Streaks. It is obvious that any difference in the speeds of two curved surfaces that move in direct contact with one another will result in a skidding or slippage of the adjacent surfaces. A layer or film of a slippery substance such as a lithographic ink on the surfaces will aggravate this tendency to skid.

If the plate cylinder on an offset press attempts to revolve faster than the contacting blanket cylinder (or vice versa), its inked surface will slip on that of the slower moving cylinder. This surface skidding causes a rupture in the film of ink on the plate or the blanket or, more likely, both. Subsequently, the rupture appears as a streak on the printed sheet. This holds equally true, of course, of roller-to-roller or roller-to-cylinder contact.

A factor sometimes responsible for faulty impression pressures—incorrect cylinder packing—also may cause slippage streaks. This occurs when, for instance, an overpacked blanket attempts to drive the plate cylinder faster than the plate cylinder gear teeth will allow it to turn. The overpacked blanket does this by surface contact, its enlarged circumference traveling at a higher rate of speed than the plate. An immediate conflict develops between the surface-contact drive of the overpacked blanket and the restraining influence of the gear teeth. The gear teeth always prove stronger than the drive or push of the inked surface of the blanket, and the blanket skids fractionally while in contact with the plate.

Ruptures in the film of ink caused by a slipping overpacked blanket cylinder will appear as streaks on the printed sheet at intervals corresponding to the pitch of the cylinder gear teeth.*

Another slippage streak caused by an overpacked blanket, but having no discernible relationship to the pitch of the gear teeth, occurs when the overpacked blanket strikes the plate cylinder during each revolution of the press. The resulting bump causes the form rollers, then in contact with the plate, to bounce and skid. This produces a rupture in the film of ink on the plate, about halfway around the cylinder.

Incorrect cylinder packing can lead to slippage streaks in still another fashion. Sometimes the flexing action of excessive impression pressures causes a blanket to work partially loose from the rear or forward clamping devices. The heavy plate-to-blanket pressure then causes a fold or wave to develop across the blanket. The wave rolls forward just ahead of the impression nip (the point of contact between two revolving cylinders) until the resiliency of the rubber causes it to snap back and skid against the plate.

Impression Cylinder Ink Build-Up. The impression cylinder surface must remain clean and smooth to insure the production of acceptably sharp prints. A periodic examination and thorough cleaning of the impression cylinder usually suffices to keep its surface free of oil, grease, dirt and the normal accumulation of dried ink. Occasionally, however, ink build-up on the impression cylinder occurs so rapidly as to result in almost immediate printing difficulties.

This happens when a heavy film of slow drying ink imprinted on the first side of a two-side job adheres to and piles up on the impression cylinder during the second printing. As the ink piles

---

Gear pitch: The interval between two gear teeth; the distance from the center-point of one gear tooth to the center-point of the next.

heavier and heavier on the impression cylinder surface, it increases the pressure between the impression cylinder and the blanket in the area or areas of ink build-up.

Since the ink build-up likely will not occur evenly, the increase in impression may vary from one area of the piling to another. As the condition worsens, random low spots appear across the printed sheets. The operator may attribute these low spots to defects in the blanket and attempt to build them up with tissue paper. This only exaggerates the problem.

Excessive build-up and subsequent drying of piled ink on the impression cylinder surface eventually *will* damage a blanket and perhaps force its repair or replacement. In many cases, serious impression cylinder ink build-up causes an embossing or actual rupturing of the printed sheets.

Impression cylinder ink build-up occurs primarily because the ink printed on the first side of a sheet has too little time to set or dry before the operator commences the second, backup printing. Slow drying of a printed ink film results from insufficient drier in the ink, from a too-heavy film of ink or because excessive water from the fountain solution has brought about a water-in-ink emulsification.

Whenever you back up a printed sheet, check the first side printed throughout the second press run. Look for odd markings, print distortions and paper embossing that did not occur on the sheet during the first printing. These telltale signs often indicate ink build-up on the impression cylinder surface.

Besides printing in thin-to-medium films of ink having adequate amounts of drier and keeping the dampening solution to a minimum, you can approach the problem of ink build-up in two other ways. Some operators reduce the impression cylinder to blanket cylinder pressure enough to permit the placement of a sheet of oiled tympan paper on the impression cylinder. The oily surface of tympan paper helps reduce the incidence of ink build-up. Securing tympan paper to the cylinder may prove difficult on some offset presses. On these machines, try periodically spraying the impression cylinder surface with silicone, Teflon or liquid graphite. This has proven effective in combatting impression cylinder ink build-up on many offset presses.

Problems with Ink

Slippage Streaks. As explained, streaks or ruptures in the print that lie across the sheet, parallel to the cylinders' axes, almost invariably happen because of roller or cylinder surface slippage. The slicker the contacting surfaces, the more likely will slippage occur.

Printing an extremely soft ink on a high-gloss paper may produce a surface slippery enough to encourage skidding. The streaks will occur directly on the sheets during impression, rather than secondarily as after a plate-to-blanket skid. On the press, the ink rupture may appear only on the blanket and not on the plate.

Although not directly the cause of blanket-to-plate skidding, a soft ink will induce slippage streaks if the blanket's surface has become glazed and smooth. Smooth, ink-glazed inking rollers similarly can lead to slippage streaks, as can fine-grained plates having large solid areas, if an extremely soft, free-flowing ink is used.

Changing to an ink having slightly more tack should prevent streaks that arise from this cause of roller or cylinder skidding. Since slippage streaks appear more noticeable with either a dark or a transparent ink, changing to an opaque or to a lighter colored ink will decrease the seriousness of a slippage streak problem.

Ink Misting. Ink misting is a condition where microscopic ink particles fly into the atmosphere from the surface of rapidly turning press rollers. A lithographic ink mists or flies primarily because it has insufficient body or viscosity — internal cohesiveness — to prevent fine ink particles from breaking loose from the film of color riding the rollers.

A tendency of an ink to mist increases as the speed of the press increases and the temperature of the ink rises. The centrifugal force developed by higher surface speeds of revolving inking rollers overcomes an ever larger percentage of the ink's cohesive strength. At the same time, roller surface friction raises the ink's temperature. This brings about a substantial decrease in the ink's normal viscosity, further impairing its resistance to molecular separation. The operator can usually minimize the effects of the problem by running the press at slower speeds when using an ink especially prone to misting.

An ink that mists will be an especially "long" ink, one fluid enough that permits drawing an amount of it out into a long, slender thread before it breaks. Sometimes an operator produces a mist-prone ink by mixing a reducing varnish into a short ink in an attempt to overcome other printing problems. Conversely, adding a heavy body gum or a more viscous varnish to an ink will diminish its tendency to mist.

Other methods of mist-control may prove even more beneficial under certain conditions. If additional coloring pigment is ground into a free-flowing ink to give it more body, the extra pigmentation increases the ink's color strength and this permits it to run in a thinner film without detracting from the appearance of the print. Running an ink in a thinner film increases its tack or stickiness, and decreases its tendency to mist. If you have a short ink of the same color strength, try mixing it with equal portions of a misting ink to control or minimize the problem. Adding a heavy-bodied white extending ink to it will reduce an ink's tendency to mist, but this also tones down the ink's color strength.

Overcome a bad misting problem and you immediately realize three benefits: a reduction of air pollutants; elimination of the dirty film of ink that overlays paper, furniture and pressroom machinery; and an end to this source of waste of lithographic inks.

Poor Ink Trapping. In wet multicolor presswork, because second, third and fourth printings occur before the complete drying of the preceding ink film(s), the tack or stickiness of each color must be greater than that of the following ink. This descending order of tack strength insures the proper trapping or holding of each color by the ink and paper it overprints, and avoids such problems as "reverse printing" where an extra tacky film of ink on the blanket strips from the paper some of the color just printed. This can happen if we should run the four colors in other than the multicolor printing sequence — yellow, red, blue and black — that these inks' formulas usually call for. If the color tones desired for a particular job require printing multicolor inks in an unusual sequence, you will achieve better results by ordering inks especially formulated for the job. Otherwise, adhere to the standard printing sequence.

On short run jobs the tack of one or more colors may be altered to permit printing in a different sequence. To print red and blue first, add to these inks a small amount of a varnish of greater viscosity than that of the varnishes already in the inks. Then slightly decrease the yellow's tack by mixing into it a less viscous varnish so you can print it third or fourth in the sequence of color laydown. Remember that these altered inks will not thereafter trap as efficiently one on another in their original printing sequence.

Usually, the first-down ink used in multicolor printing will have a high color strength. This permits printing it in a relatively thin film, desirable because the greater tack of a thin film of ink traps better than that of a thick film of ink. Trapping difficulties in multicolor presswork often result from printing the first-down inks in relatively thick films that fail to trap efficiently.

In dry multicolor printing, where the first-down ink is permitted to set or partially dry before the second-down color is printed, trapping difficulties can arise because of additives contained in the first-down ink. For instance, ink manufacturers often add wax to a metallic ink to retard vehicle penetration into the printing surface. As a printed film of metallic ink dries, any wax it contains precipitates from the vehicle and hardens into a thin, transparent coating over the ink's surface. This film of wax interferes with the trapping of any ink printed over the metallic ink; as it dries, a second-down ink may easily rub off wherever it has overprinted a wax-impregnated ink.

Mottle. Ink mottle, a blotchy or spotty condition of the printed ink film, shows up most noticeably in halftone and solid areas of the print. The printed material often appears to have been subjected to an unpatterned splattering of large water drops.

Perhaps the most common cause of ink mottle in offset printing is water-in-ink emulsion or waterlogging. Running excessive fountain solution to the dampening rollers eventually overcomes a lithographic ink's resistance to admixture with water. As the water content of an ink rises, the ink loses considerable tack, or internal cohesiveness. During impression, the ink squashes unevenly onto the surface of the material being printed. The operator's initial reaction to the appearance of ink mottle should be to check and correct the ink/water balance by cutting back on the water feed.

Ink mottle may be encountered when printing a heavy film of low viscosity ink on a hard, non-absorbent surface. Here again, the ink tends to squash unevenly onto the printing surface during impression. To overcome the difficulty, switch to an ink having a high color density and run a thin film of color to the inking rollers.

Printing a deep penetrating ink on some cheaper grades of paper occasionally results in "absorption mottle." Because of the variable texture of these papers, ink may penetrate deeper into some small, irregularly shaped areas than it does into nearby areas of the paper's surface. Changing to a different paper or running a high color strength, high viscosity ink in a thin film will end the problem.

Absorption mottle appears more pronounced when it occurs with a transparent ink. A quick drawdown of two or three samples of transparent inks shows that these inks yield different color strengths between thin and thick films. When some portions of a printed ink film absorb deeply into the printing surface, these areas will have appreciably thinner coverages than other areas of the print. With a transparent ink, the apparent difference in color strength between thick and thin films of ink will seem quite marked. A similar effect often occurs when a transparent ink is printed on a paper having a rough, uneven surface, where impression pressures fail to lay down an even film of ink all across the printing surface.

Absorption mottle, and ink mottle caused or aggravated by transparent inks, uneven printing surfaces, low viscosity inks or water-in-ink emulsion, often diminish with a simple correction of impression pressures. In most cases, ink mottle will subside when impression pressure is backed off; occasionally, as when printing on an uneven surface, increasing the pressure slightly will iron or press color smoothly into the valleys and depressions of the printing surface.

Dampening Problems

High/Low pH. The pH or acid level of a lithographic fountain solution should fall between 3.8 or 4.0 and 5.5 or 6.0 on the pH acidity scale. A reading outside these lines of demarcation indicates an imbalance of fountain solution acidity. An imbalance of acidity, especially where a low pH reading indicates excess acid in the solution, can lead to such problems as plate scumming, plate blinding, roller stripping and poor drying of the printed ink film.

When prepared as directed by the manufacturer, a batch of fountain solution will have the pH value correct for the plate in use, provided:

— —water reasonably free of chemical and mineral impurities is used;

— —precise amounts of water, gum arabic, solution concentrate and necessary additives are mixed together in clean, accurate measuring beakers;

— —the water fountain and all the dampening system rollers are clean and cannot impregnate thé fresh solution with ink, dirt or other impurities;

— —the fresh solution is not added to old solution of questionable quality.

Any one or a combination of these often unsuspected causitive factors can give rise to a pH imbalance. To mention one, a serious pH imbalance may develop because of chemicals or minerals in the city water used to prepare fountain solutions. The chemical and mineral composition of municipal water in different localities currently meets no set standard. Those in charge of city water supplies have the responsibility for providing water fit for human consumption, not water suitable for use in lithographic pressrooms.

A printing difficulty may come on unexpectedly when a mineral or chemical suddenly appears in municipal water normally free of such material. When this occurs, the most careful measurements of ingredients may not prevent a solution pH imbalance. To prevent contamination by unfiltered ingredients in the water, technicians recommend using distilled water when preparing lithographic fountain solutions.

Plate Scumming. A general scumming condition over large non-image areas of the press plate usually indicates too little moisture is reaching the plate's surface. Without adequate moisture, these areas dry out and begin to accept ink. Often scumming will appear on the plate in bands of varying widths running in the direction of cylinder movement. A close inspection of scumming may reveal an imprintor duplication of the weave of the dampening roller cover fabric.

Besides the more obvious causes of plate scumming— improper platemaking procedures, use of an ink that readily scums and running insufficient moisture to the dampening system — the follo also may cause scumming problems to develop.

Improperly set or dirty dampener rollers give rise to scumming that continues until we take the necessary corrective action. Dirty or ink-surfaced dampener roller covers will quickly create or contribute to a scumming situation. Remove a dampener roller from the press for thorough cleaning the instant he encounters any dirtiness that refuses to depart the roller's cover extra water is sponged onto the roller. Since this usually occurs in the middle of a press run, you will save time if you have previously readied a spare set of dampener rollers by wetting them down with fountain solution or water. The dampened spares will be ready to place on the press at a moment's notice.

Worn or baggy roller covers that readily accept ink will induce or encourage scumming. Examine the covers periodically and replace them before trouble develops, if possible.

The plate scumming called mourning-band scum usually develops because of insufficient moisture. Mourning-band scum occurs in dark bands along both sides of the press plate. Mourning bands or "widow bands" often develop when the form dampening rollers prove inadequate to the task of supplying sufficient moisture to the outside edges of an overwide plate. Newer dampening systems having longer rollers that distribute ample moisture to all areas of the plate prevent or mitigate the occurrence of mourning-band scum. On an older press, the operator may have to use plates with all image areas falling well within the plate-edge trouble zone.

The second cause of mourning-band scum, sometimes indirectly related to the dampening system but more often to washup practices, involves the swelling of the outside edges of plate or blanket packing sheets. This brings extra pressure to bear on these areas. Because continued excessive pressure at any point on an offset plate will cause serious wear, avoid packing-sheet swell through strict control of the water supply and careful washup practices and by cutting the packing sheets no wider than the plate or blanket.

Roller Stripping. Roller stripping — where the inking rollers reject ink in narrow bands around their circumferences — can arise either from running excessive moisture to the dampening systems or from the use of an improperly formulated fountain solution, as well as from the physical condition of the rollers, largely controlled by proper washup practices.

During the operation of an offset press an unavoidable competition develops between the ink and the water at their point of contact on the inking rollers. The water continually attempts to supplant the film of ink. The greatest conflict occurs on the steel vibrator rollers and metal distributing drums. If enough moisture is admitted to the dampening system to overcome the ink's resistance to supplantation by water, the fountain solution will desensitize the inking rollers. As this continues, the rollers become increasingly water receptive and ink repellant, until a roller stripping condition develops. To avoid the problem, maintain a correct ink/water balance.

An improperly formulated fountain solution, especially a solution containing excessive amounts of gum arabic or phosphoric acid, increases the solution's tendency to drive ink from the inking rollers. If we add a desensitizing etch to a solution to counteract the effects of an ink that persists in scumming, we may inadvertently bring about a roller stripping condition. If roller stripping develops during a press run examine and, if necessary, replace the dampening solution.

A glazed condition of their surfaces will encourage stripping of inking rollers; keep the rollers free of glaze and maintain them in a pliable, ink-receptive condition through a workable system of roller cleaning to help prevent the problem.

Dampener and Ink Roller Maintenance

Dampening Rollers and Dampener Roller Covers. The close control of moisture delivered to the plate surface requires that all the rollers in the dampening system remain in the best possible condition. Torn, loose or tightly twisted roller covers cannot efficiently take up and release fountain solution in a steady, undeviating flow. Ink-filled covers, in addition to rejecting water, quickly condition non-image areas of the plate to accept ink. Whether the dampening system carries too much or too little moisture, several printing problems can develop as a result of defective dampener roller covers.

Only periodic inspections of the dampening rollers will keep the operator aware of their condition. Give the roller covers at least a brief examination at washup time. Make sure that incorrect mounting has not permitted the outer cover to slip back from the ends of a roller. This inhibits a roller's ability to carry adequate amounts of moisture, mourning-band scum being the most probable consequence. An excessively worn, ragged or torn cover or one that hangs loosely from the roller will also cause difficulties. Replace such a cover before attempting to use the roller again.

While replacing a dampening roller's outer cover, inspect the second cover layer. This second layer of cover material acts as a water reservoir to keep the plate-contacting outer layer wet with a continuous and even supply of fountain solution. The second layer should fit tight and snug along the entire length of the roller. It should not sag, bulge or wrinkle and should be free of large tears and rips. Its fabric should not hold large amounts of dried ink that prevent acceptance and retention of moisture. If an examination reveals any of these defects, remove this important second layer of covering material for replacement. At this time, inspect any third layer of covering material the roller may carry for possible need of replacement.

When it is necessary to remove all the cover layers of a dampener roller for replacement, take time to assess the condition of the basic rubber stock of the roller. With a machinist's caliper, or other precise instrument, measure the roller's diameter from one end to the other. Its diameter should not vary more than a few thousandths of an inch. The rubber stock of an old dampener roller may swell at each end. If it does, this could be the source of uneven dampening of the plate. Send the roller to the manufacturer for regrinding or replacement.

Ink Rollers. The operator of an offset press should regularly check the condition of all the inking rollers in current use. A close examination of the rollers' ends will disclose any serious checking or cracking, a condition that signals the onset of roller deterioration and frequently results in the appearance of roller-particle hickies in the printed image.

Unusual plate wear or damage can result when a sharp, hard particle becomes imbedded in an inking roller. The particle will scratch a line through the protective film and into the base metal of the plate. A hairline "rule" then appears on the printed sheet. When such a defect shows up, inspect the form rollers with the aid of a magnifying glass. This will help locate small pieces of metal, wood or other slivers of foreign matter imbedded in the roller surface. Carefully remove these from the roller with a needle or a sharpened stylus.

Check the inking rollers for uniform roundness with a caliper or by placing two rollers side by side on a light table; light visible between the rollers indicates one or both of them lack the necessary uniform roundness to insure proper ink distribution.

Badly cracked rollers, rollers that have become chewed up by pieces of metal or other sharp material, and rollers markedly out-of-round probably should be replaced. The operator will find old, deteriorating rollers difficult if not impossible to renew by cleaning alone. Even a vigorous pumice-powder scrubbing will not rejuvenate badly cracked roller ends.

If the damage does not seem too severe, or if an out-of-round roller is only slightly off true, the roller usually can be renewed through a process of factory regrinding. Consult with your supplier of offset press inking rollers concerning his services of roller renewal.

One cause of roller-related printing difficulties, so obvious as to be largely overlooked, involves the system of roller replacement followed by the operator. In many printing plants new rollers remain in their shipping crate or stored in a rack until long after they are needed on the press. But continued production of high quality printing demands that the roller *on the press* be the best rollers available to the operator.

A compromise system of roller rotation developed by technicians years ago works as well today in keeping all the inking rollers on an offset press in good working order and insuring that a new or next-to-new roller always occupies the most important position in the train of rollers in the inking system.

Select the best roller available, a new roller if possible, and place it at the forward position in the chain of inking rollers. Designate this roller as roller No. 1. Behind roller No. 1, install rollers No. 2, 3 and 4, with each roller progressively older and more worn.

Roller No. 4, the one showing the greatest deterioration, will be the roller to watch most carefully. When this roller becomes so badly worn as to need replacing, remove it and put roller No. 3 in its place. Move roller No. 2 into the position vacated by roller No. 3 and move roller No. 1 back one space.

Now put a new roller in the position formerly occupied by roller No. 1. The new roller becomes roller No. 1; old roller No. 1 becomes roller No. 2, and so on. Again, roller No. 4 will be the oldest and most worn of the group, riding in the least critical position on the press. The new roller, in its forward, plate-contacting position, will afford the best coverage and ink distribution for high quality presswork.

Unusually rapid wear of ink rollers can occur if all or part of a roller is permitted to run dry (free of ink) during operation of the press. This may happen with a large, multi-unit press when the operator uses only one unit for printing, but leaves the other unit(s) engaged. On a smaller offset press, the operator may wish to keep ink off the roller ends if the image areas lie largely in the center of the plate. In either case, operating a press for extended periods with ink roller surfaces devoid of ink eventually will lead to roller disintegration because of the heat generated by constant friction.

On a small press, an operator pressed for time may pinch off ink fed to the ends of the rollers by drawing the ink fountain blade tightly against the fountain roller. This not only leads to a rapid wearing of the roller surfaces, but as the fountain roller turns in contact with the fountain blade, it slowly grinds down the edge of the blade until correct setting of the blade becomes impossible.

To avoid the problem of overheated rollers, technicians recommend the use of a commercial lubricating material in conjunction with fountain dividers. Discuss the problem with your ink maker who can provide suitable roller surface lubricants. To use, place an amount of the colorless lubricant in the fountain where you wish the rollers to remain free of ink, and separate the lubricant from the ink supply with fountain dividers. Feed enough lubricant to the rollers to prevent blade-to-fountain roller contact.

In the case of a multi-unit press, spreading an amount of roller lubricant (or other suitable material) across uninking ink rollers of a printing unit will prevent friction and excessive heat build-up during operation of the press.

Roller lubricant performs four important functions. It prevents wear to the fountain blade. It equalizes roller surface wear. It minimizes water build-up on uninked areas of the plate. It keeps distributing ink confined to the plate's image areas.

Chapter 15
Safety in the
Offset Pressroom

One of the obstacles in the way of establishing a practical program of plant safety is the attitude of the worker or workers most directly involved. This remains true in spite of the federal Occupational Safety and Health Act (OSHA) passed by Congress in 1970, and the mountain of material since written about health, safety, and accident prevention that it has generated.

Too many workers, including many in the graphic arts industry, still tend to reject accident prevention programs developed by management. Some believe an employer's concern for loss of production and possible damage to expensive machinery overshadows his concern for employee safety and well-being. Others feel companies promote strict safety programs only to secure lower industrial accident insurance rates. Although a company probably will realize these highly desirable benefits through a program of accident prevention, a sincere concern for their workers' health and safety today motivates employers as it never has before.

The individual worker involved in an accident stands to lose far more than the employer. Other segments of the work force can make up production time losses. Management may in some cases be able to write off as a tax loss a heavily damaged piece of equipment. An emergency telephone call may suffice to bring forth a dozen applicants ready to fill in for a disabled worker. But a severed hand or arm cannot be satisfactorily replaced. Mechanical devices, no matter how easily controlled, never substitute adequately for missing arms, hands or fingers. Features badly disfigured by flames never again appear the same to their owner.

These statements may seem harsh and uncompromising. If they serve to channel thinking along lines conducive to personal involvement in plant safety, they will have served a good purpose.

For it has been estimated that while approximately 15% of all industrial accidents result from unsafe conditions, the rest stem from unsafe practices or activities of people.

We need to discover motivation that will stimulate us and those we work with to embrace wholeheartedly any health and safety program introduced. Such motivation does exist. It involves simply the development by each employee of a real and enduring concern for the health, safety and well-being of his or her co-workers. We can and should develop this concern. It will influence us so that we remain keenly aware of hazards and possible areas of danger to others, if not to ourselves. Oftentimes we more quickly notice when an unsafe condition or practice threatens a fellow worker. A desire to see others adequately protected from potential hazards, easily developed by any worker, will help insure plant safety for all.

To fully realize the benefits of any safety program, all concerned must develop a positive attitude toward accident prevention. Every worker should strive to disabuse himself or herself of any cynicism regarding an employer's health and safety programs. If an unsafe condition or practice is noticed, personally see to it that this condition or practice is changed or abolished or brought to the attention of the supervisor responsible for the plant's safety program.

Plant safety in an offset pressroom primarily concerns itself with activities of work conducted at the press and with the various chemicals used in lithography. The following material deals with pertinent press- and chemical-related activities.

Safety at the Machine

Clothing and Footwear: Any article of clothing that hangs down from an arm, the neck, the waist or a leg may become trapped in a moving part of an offset press. An extremely loose or ragged sleeve that catches between two rollers on the press easily can pull a hand or arm into the machine. Pants with deep cuffs or threadbare pants or pants' legs that dangle in such a way as to catch a part of the press or cause the operator to trip provide an ever present danger to the unwary. The same can be said for flaring or ruffled skirts and loose, baggy sweaters. Old shoes badly in need of repair can cause a fatal misstep or trip an employee up at precisely the wrong moment. Unless snugly secured beneath a jacket, vest, shirt or blouse, no long tie or string of beads should be worn around machinery of any kind. Wrist watches, as well as heavily decorated rings and bracelets, present another potential hazard; remove these and lay them aside during working hours.

The offset press operator who conscientiously wears suitable clothing and footwear runs less risk of experiencing a serious accident. Consider only neat, tidy clothing and footwear in good repair suitable for wear at work around any offset press.

Special Safety and Protective Equipment: In addition to clothing suitable for normal pressroom activities, workers also should wear special protective equipment, whenever advisable, to guard against unusual dangers. In many cases OSHA regulations require an employer to make available to workers the protective equipment needed. Only genuine employee cooperation and willing participation in the safety program in effect, however, will insure their consistent use.

Special protective clothing and other gear used in offset pressrooms include safety glasses or goggles, respirators, rubber gloves, ear plugs or ear muffs, steel reinforced safety shoes and, in rare instances, protective headgear or "hard hats." Protective devices and safety equipment of this nature prevent countless thousands of serious injuries when worn under circumstances of hazardous working conditions. Make it a point to obtain the required article of protective gear or clothing and to wear it whenever and wherever sound safety practices warrant.

Horseplay: Do not encourage, condone or participate in any type of rough horseplay in the vicinity of any press in operation. Even milder forms of horseplay, such as throwing wet sponges and paper balls, have no place in the offset pressroom. More violent forms of practical jokery — throwing waterbags, pushing or shoving, activating air hoses at unsuspecting backsides — frequently have proven extremely harmful in themselves.

Every member of the offset press crew needs to remain alert to the immediate surroundings, not only to prevent the development of expensive printing problems but to avoid the everyday hazards commonly encountered. Anything that would distract a press operator's attention from the business at hand can and often will lead to a serious accident.

The plant safety director, pressroom foreman or other person responsible, should have prominently posted in the pressroom well-defined rules against horseplay and practical jokes.

Work Habits: Work habits include practically any activity legitimately performed by employees in conjunction with their work. It may help illustrate what is meant by potentially unsafe work habits to comment on some specifically applicable to offset pressrooms.

First off, never make adjustments to any *moving* part of a press in operation. Too often, insufficient working room exists around the adjustment device to permit free and easy access to it without endangering fingers or a hand. Whenever an adjustment is made to (a non-moving part of) a machine in operation, avoid touching either the machine or the adjustment device until at a complete and fully balanced stop directly in front of the part on which you plan to work. Have each foot firmly planted on a solid surface. Never touch any part of a press in operation while moving toward it or away from it, or use the machine for balance while walking around it or past it.

In this respect, while working on or near a press, whether it is shut off or in operation, avoid balancing or supporting yourself precariously on the machine. A sudden slip and heavy fall onto or into the press, or against any of its sharp projections, can cause a serious accident.

When removing printed sheets from the press delivery for inspection, do not rush the operation. Until thoroughly accustomed to the mechanics of sheet removal from an unfamiliar press, run the machine at a speed slow enough to permit safe removal of the sheets. Continually observe the running sheets, the moving delivery bars and your hand as it enters the delivery. A slight lifting or lowering of a hand may cause a missed sheet and leave fingers exposed to delivery bar grippers. If a sheet buckles and it crumples in the delivery, or if sheets crumple up in the delivery for other reasons, stop the machine to remove or realign the sheets. This will prove both quicker and safer and will result in fewer sheets being spoiled.

Remember to perform all press oiling and cleaning operations only with the machine stopped and the drive motor switched off. This simple safety practice prevents a great many injuries to fingers, hands, arms and eyes. It also prevents damage to the press. A metal oil spout or thick wad of cleaning rag can easily become caught between moving parts of the press and either be whipped into the air or jam the machine and put it out of commission.

Do not form the habit of eating food in the immediate working area of an offset press. Eating at a work station may cause ingestion of a small amount of a poisonous solvent or dangerous chemical with every bite taken. Keep fingers away from the mouth at all times except immediately after having washed them thoroughly with soap and water. Solvent contaminated fingers, common in modern offset pressrooms, constitute a real if invisible danger to lithographers.

Aisles, Walkways and Footboards: Keep all aisles and walking or standing surfaces between presses, along workbenches and around tables clean and free of grease, oil, ink and other spilled liquids, oily rags,* wet sponges and waste sheets. Keep the footboards and "catwalks" on or near each press equally clean and free of slippery substances and materials. The importance of this is seen when it is realized that of all the industrial accidents that occur, a substantial majority of them result from unsafe walking and standing surfaces.

The walking areas and aisleways between presses and across the pressroom should whenever possible follow straight lines and have no "blind" corners. Keep the aisles open and uncluttered. Avoid congesting them with stacks or rolls of paper, paper skids and wheeled paper lifts, tables, tool boxes, scattered tools and other pressroom equipment. Low-profile objects over which a person may trip create hazards in any walkway or work area. Brightly colored

---

Good safety regulations require the availability and use in printing plant pressrooms of fireproof metal containers for the safe storage of dirty or oily rags and solvent/ink-impregnated pressrags. Each container should have a strong, tight-fitting lid.

stripes painted on the floor to outline aisles and walkways help remind everyone concerned to avoid generating aisle or walkway clutter.

Lifting and Carrying: Many injuries of a serious and permanent nature that occur to industrial workers result from the incorrect lifting of heavy objects, or from trying to lift items too heavy for one person. All pressroom personnel should learn and use the correct methods for lifting heavy articles. No one should attempt to lift anything beyond his or her capacity. Whenever possible, use the hoists, lift trucks, paper carts and other mechanical devices provided for lifting and transporting.

Avoiding carrying paper or other material stacked in your arms high enough to obstruct your vision. Place large amounts of cut paper on a cart or if necessary take two or more trips to transport it by hand to and from the pressroom area. Otherwise, the worker risks tripping over or bumping into unseen objects left in an aisle or walkway.

Machine Guards: Most offset presses have metal or wire guards and covers that prevent the operator's fingers from approaching the danger zone around gears, wheels and belts. In order to clean, adjust or repair a press one or more of these guards may need to be removed. Always replace them before putting the machine back into operation.

If a belt or set of gears on a press lacks a safety guard, investigate the feasibility of having one constructed and installed on the machine. Be sure that such a guard does not in itself create a hazard by having sharp projections or ragged, cutting edges. Avoid cluttering the press with Jerry-rigged devices of limited utility and questionable safety. Other machines such as drills, lathes, saws and air compressors that might occupy space in the pressroom also need adequate protective guards, shields and covers.

Compressed Air and Air Hoses: Many pressrooms have one of the familiar air compressors, with its coiled rubber hose and brass nozzle, that workers utilize for various cleaning purposes. At this writing, OSHA regulations prohibit the use of air pressure above 30 psi (pounds per square inch). Higher pressures present a hazard to workers by causing small, hard particles of dirt or metal to fly or ricochet across the pressroom.

Adequate safety precautions call for a worker to wear adequate protective glasses or goggles while using a compressed air hose. Inspect the hose periodically for breaks or weakened areas, especially around the metal fittings.

Electric Wiring: Wiring for modern offset pressrooms should provide for the grounding of any electric motor, power tool or electrically driven machine that has bare metal subject to exposure to a damp or occasionally wet environment. Before plugging in or operating any electrical equipment, make sure the power cord has a third (ground) wire correctly grounded to the unit.

If a press or other piece of equipment lacks proper grounding, have a qualified electrician do the work necessary to ground it.

Inspect wires and power cords frequently and have replaced any that show badly worn or frayed areas. Do not use spliced electrical wiring or power cords. Under no circumstances should a nest of power cords drawing electricity from one electric outlet be permitted.

Misuse of electrical wiring has resulted in far too many fires for any of us to take these admonitions lightly. In the offset pressroom, where fumes from flammable solvents and chemicals many accumulate to a dangerous extent, there exists a special hazard of flash fires and explosions caused by sparks from shorted wiring.

Smoking: In many places of work, industrial safety directors hesitate to mention the special hazards attending the use of cigarettes, much less take the often highly unpopular step of posting "No Smoking" signs. Too many workers given to smoking resent this supposed abrogation of personal rights. This is unfortunate.

In the offset pressroom, smoking—or more specifically the cigarette spark and match flame it entails—is a special safety hazard. In the presence of the fumes from the safest of cleaning solvents, a burning match or lighted cigarette can cause an explosion or flash fire. Since the introduction of alcohol into offset press dampening solutions, care with fire from whatever source has assumed greater importance than ever before.

If the employer or supervisor places a ban on smoking in the pressroom, for everyone's safety, abide by the no-smoking rule. It will not kill anyone; ignoring the rule might. In the absence of a no-smoking rule, we would do well to have enough respect for the highly flammable and combustible solvents, chemicals and other materials used in offset pressrooms to forsake the habit voluntarily during working hours. Be safe. Those whose smoke should do so during coffee breaks, lunch periods or before and after work.

Press and Pressroom Familiarity: One of the first things for a new member of the pressroom crew to learn in conjunction with a safety program is the location and operation of all power switches, first-aid and safety equipment and to know the location of any list of emergency telephone numbers.

In addition, as soon as practicable, every worker directly concerned with the machines should become familiar enough with each press to know how to turn it off, release the rollers, throw off the impression pressures and move the machine through its cycle by hand. If an operator gets a finger or hand caught in a press, this will insure the expenditure of the least amount of time in getting the injured person free from the press.

When an accident does occur, call or send for assistance, leaving the injured person alone no longer than absolutely necessary. Make the injured person as comfortable as possible and treat for shock before applying first aid treatment or while awaiting the arrival of competent medical help.

A realistic safety program obviously calls for one or more members of the pressroom crew on each shift of work to have safety and first-aid training and to know the location of available emergency equipment (medication, tourniquets, stretcher, wheel chair) and how to use it. The plant should have a plan of operation that an emergency situation itself will activate. A plan that spells out in detail the procedure to take in case of emergency, conspicuously posted in the pressroom, will prove invaluable.

Safe Handling of Lithographic Chemicals

A wide variety of solvents, chemicals and chemical mixtures passes through the modern offset or lithographic pressroom. The use of some of these materials involves risks potentially dangerous to workers. The dangers include internal poisoning, lung inflammation or infection, skin irritations and fire, which also can cause extensive damage to machinery, shop furniture and buildings. In order to insure a safe and reasonably healthy working environment, all who handle lithographic chemicals must follow certain basic safety principles.

Proper storage of the chemicals and solvents used in an offset pressroom should rank high in importance on any health and safety program. Keep all toxic and all flammable liquids tightly sealed in airtight containers from which potentially harmful or dangerous fumes cannot escape. Make sure every container of a lithographic chemical displays a label that clearly reveals its contents. Never pour a chemical or solvent into an unmarked container or into a container that bears an erroneous label. To avoid accidental poisoning, never use a milk carton, soda pop bottle, drinking glass or any other food container to mix, weigh or store any solvent or chemical.

Store flammable liquids and chemicals and all toxic substances in a safe place well away from any work area. Keep volatile solvents and chemicals away from heaters, electric motors and out of direct sunlight. The storeroom or storage area should have ample walking, standing and turning room between shelves and between containers, crates or boxes that occupy floor space. Adequate illumination in the storage area aids in the proper selection of different materials and helps prevent accidents that may arise from using or mixing together the wrong chemicals.

In a storage area provided with shelving, store liquid and powder-form chemicals on the lowest possible shelves. Avoid placing containers of potentially harmful chemicals on a high shelf from which they may drop or spill onto a person standing below. Spills of corrosive chemicals that occur on lower shelves cause the least amount of damage to other material kept in the storeroom.

OSHA regulations now set limits on the amounts of so-called Class A liquids we may store in a working area. The safe amounts of a volatile substance stored in a given area may vary according to the size of the area and the volatility of the chemical. Refer to the proper OSHA regulations for a specific product. Volatile or flammable liquids such as benzene, naphtha, isopropyl alcohol and similar solvents or chemicals having a flashpoint* below 100° F.

The lowest temperature at which the vapors or fumes from a volatile substance will ignite in the presence of a spark or flame.

make up the group of Class A liquids. For general shop safety, unless otherwise specified, limit the amount of such chemicals kept in a working area to that required for one shift of work.

The actual handling of lithographic chemicals — measuring, mixing, pouring — also requires some thought and considerable care on the part of the worker. Always wear protective rubber gloves or the solvent-resistant gloves recommended by the chemical manufacturer when handling fountain solution concentrates, strong solvents and other harsh liquids. This prevents the onset of dermatitis. Wearing a rubber apron or protective shop coat will keep spilled liquids from soaking into clothing that directly contacts the skin.

Clearly written information detailing further specific precautions to take with a particularly dangerous solvent or chemical should appear on the applicable container. This information should include recommended additional protective clothing or equipment a worker should wear while handling the material, safe handling procedures and storage requirements, and proper cleaning or decontamination action to take in case of spillage or leakage of the container's contents. First-aid or other emergency measures that prevent skin rash, blistering and burning, or fatal poisoning also should appear on containers. Federal law also requires a label or warning sticker that carries specific data as to the ingested toxic limit of a poisonous substance or pertinent eye-, nasal- and skin-contact information to appear on some products. If this information appears on any container of potentially harmful material, take time to study it before opening the container.

For general handling, storage and use safety, you should in addition have readily available information concerned with a solvent's or chemical's flashpoint in closed or open containers, evaporation rate, vapor density, the safe limit of concentration of these vapors in the pressroom atmosphere, the liquid's boiling point, its specific gravity (which indicates whether vapors from a liquid tend to collect near the floor of the pressroom or disperse into the air conditioning system), and whether or not the danger of spontaneous combustion exists.

Besides the foregoing data, every container of a solvent or chemical (liquid or powder) should have explicit directions for its mixture with other materials and the proper methods for its application. Many industrial accidents have occurred simply because a worker mixed together the wrong chemicals, mixed chemicals in incorrect proportions, or used the product in the wrong way. It is, of course, a worker's responsibility to read, understand and follow the directions for its use that are printed on a container of a lithographic solvent or chemical.

General safety instructions for the proper mixing and preparation of all chemicals apply to those used in offset pressrooms. Make it an iron-clad habit to pour the specified portion of a chemical concentrate into the necessary amount of water when mixing up any solution. Especially avoid pouring water into a container that holds an acid. Avoid looking down into any tumbler, beaker, jar or bottle while pouring a solvent, chemical or chemical solution into it. Rising fumes or splashing liquid easily can prove harmful to the face, the eyes or the lungs.

Avoid prolonged skin contact with any lithographic chemical, no matter how mild it may be. Wash hands frequently to keep them clean and free of chemical residues. If a strong, burning chemical comes in contact with your hands, face or neck, immediately wash the affected area with plenty of soap and water. A mild lotion, salve or cream worked into the skin will replace the natural oils removed by washing and will prevent painful chapping. If a chemical splashes into your eyes, rinse them thoroughly with clear water, then seek appropriate and immediate medical attention.

Many of the chemical products used in an offset pressroom charge the atmosphere with toxic fumes through evaporation. Some vapors constitute a greater hazard to human health than others. Federal regulations have established "threshold limit values of airborne contaminants" for evaporative chemicals and solvents to serve as a basis for controlling the percentages of toxic vapors present in a given working area. We may deem "safe" a mildly toxic vapor at an atmospheric concentration of 1000 ppm*, while a more toxic substance may prove harmful at concentrations above 200 ppm.

Information accompanying every solvent or chemical that enters an offset pressroom should include its "threshold limit" rating. Airborne contaminants and toxic vapor concentrations from the material should never rise above the established safe limit.

This may require initial and periodic testing, by technicians from an industrial laboratory equipped to make such tests, of samples of air taken from different work areas in the pressroom and around the presses. The technicians, or the pressroom safety directory can use the results of these tests to determine if procedural changes or material substitution might bring about a lowering of vapor concentrations to a safer level.

Often a simple substitution of one solvent or chemical for another will eliminate or substantially mitigate a potential health hazard. For instance, the normal propyl alcohol (safety rating: 200 ppm) used in many offset press fountain solutions should be replaced with isopropyl alcohol, which has a safe allowable atmospheric concentration of 400 ppm. Isopropyl performs as efficiently as normal propyl alcohol, while posing approximately half the threat to a worker's health. Some materials such as carbon tetrachloride (safety rating: 10 ppm) should be avoided altogether. "Carbon tet" may cause irreparable damage to lungs, livers and kidneys. Prolonged exposure to this hazardous substance in an area lacking sufficient ventilation can result in death. Substituting almost any good proprietary cleaning agent for carbon tetrachloride improves the atmospheric condition of the work area.

Where unsafe concentration levels exist, and solvent or chemical substitutions cannot be made, workers should wear OSHA-approved respirators, gas masks or other protective equipment when handling highly toxic substances.

By no means do lithographic chemicals present hazards that make working in offset pressrooms unusually dangerous. The chemical hazard factor in the graphic arts field in general and in offset pressrooms in particular compares favorably with similar

---

Vapor or particulate concentration in the atmosphere of an evaporative substance is expressed in "parts per million." At a concentration of 500 ppm, 500 cubic centimenters (cc) of a substance in the form of airborne particulates or contaminants have impregnated one million cc of the surrounding atmosphere. Whether a particular atmospheric concentration of a vaporized substance will prove dangerous to those working in the area largely depends upon the toxicity of the vapors.

work areas in other industries. If we continue to update and strive to implement sound safety programs, we can maintain this position of relative safety for pressroom personnel. A little extra effort directed along these lines, by both employers and employees, easily could see offset pressrooms ranked among the safest work areas in the U.S. It is a goal well worth working toward.

Index